Studies in the Evolution
of Industrial Society

KENNIKAT PRESS SCHOLARLY REPRINTS

Dr. Ralph Adams Brown, Senior Editor

Series on
ECONOMIC THOUGHT, HISTORY AND CHALLENGE
Under the General Editorial Supervision of
Dr. Sanford D. Gordon
Professor of Economics, State University of New York

Studies in the Evolution of Industrial Society

BY

RICHARD T. ELY, Ph.D., LL.D.

Volume I

KENNIKAT PRESS
Port Washington, N. Y./London

STUDIES IN THE EVOLUTION OF INDUSTRIAL SOCIETY

First published in 1903
Reissued in 1971 by Kennikat Press
Library of Congress Catalog Card No: 78-137940
ISBN 0-8046-1443-1

Manufactured by Taylor Publishing Company   Dallas, Texas

KENNIKAT SERIES ON ECONOMIC THOUGHT,
HISTORY AND CHALLENGE

This Book is Dedicated to

MR. JUSTICE OLIVER WENDELL HOLMES

Of the Supreme Court of the United States

IN APPRECIATION OF THE ENLIGHTENED PHILOSOPHY
SO CONSPICUOUS IN HIS OPINIONS, WHICH IS LAYING
A FIRM FOUNDATION FOR A SUPERSTRUCTURE
OF INDUSTRIAL LIBERTY

PREFACE

THE following words were used in the "Editor's Preface" to the Citizen's Library of Economics, Politics, and Sociology : " It is the conviction of the Editor that scientific work in the field of the humanities may generally be made interesting to intelligent citizens through cultivation of clearness in statement and literary style. . . . It is desired to lay emphasis on the fact that while the sciences of Economics, Politics, and Sociology are of concern to the citizen and make appropriate the title 'Citizen's Library,' in no case will the interests of science be sacrificed to popularity. The aim will be to bring every volume in the Library up to the present standard of science, and it is hoped that the Library will in more than one instance push forward the boundaries of knowledge." These words express the ideal which the author has kept before him in the preparation of the present volume. This statement is made, not because the author ventures to hope that he has fully attained his ideal, but because the statement of the purpose which has constantly been kept in view may prove helpful to the reader. Many difficult topics are discussed in these pages, and an immense field is traversed. This field belongs largely to that general borderland where economics, ethics, biology, and sociology meet. At the same time, in its preparation the writer has never forgotten that he is writing as an economist. This borderland will surely prove scientifically fruitful territory, and it must be worked by men who approach it from the viewpoint of the different sciences mentioned. If the work is well done in each case, the scientific products will vary, but will constitute an harmonious whole.

A list is appended of the author's articles and published addresses which have been used to a greater or less extent in this volume, and the author makes his acknowledgments with thanks to the publishers for permission to reprint. Notwithstanding the fact that the list is a rather long one, the book is essentially new. A large part of it has never appeared in print before, and even when previous articles have been used, they have generally been greatly altered and enlarged. The style of a speaker addressing an audience is preserved in the papers on "Competition; its Nature, it Permanency, and its Beneficence" and "Industrial Liberty," which the author delivered as presi-

PREFACE

dent of the American Economic Association in the years 1900 and 1901 respectively. Although elsewhere the author speaks in the third person, there seemed to him more to be gained than lost by so doing.

The general plan of the book is probably made sufficiently obvious by a perusal of the Table of Contents. Part I gives a general survey of the evolution of industrial society; Part II treats specific problems which are problems of industrial evolution. These problems are all suggested in Part I, and they are distinctively problems which have been the outcome of industrial evolution. This thought of industrial evolution has been constantly kept in mind, and gives unity to the book.

The author is well aware that there is scarcely a chapter in the book which could not be expanded into a volume. He hopes, however, that he has been able to keep a due proportion between the various topics discussed, and that by following this method he has been able to lay a foundation for future work.

Acknowledgments for valuable suggestions are due to Professors J. Mark Baldwin, Charles J. Bullock, Thomas N. Carver, Frank A. Fetter, Franklin H. Giddings, E. A. Ross, and to Dr. G. R. Wicker.

PREFACE

The author's acknowledgments are due to Mr. Solomon Huebner, Graduate Scholar in Economics, for permission to use the excellent tables of inheritance tax legislation in foreign countries, which he has prepared as part of a thorough monographic treatment of modern inheritance taxation. Finally, it is the author's duty and pleasure to express his appreciation for the varied assistance given him by his colleague, Mr. Max O. Lorenz, Assistant in Economics. The untiring and very efficient efforts of Mr. Lorenz have lightened his labors and added to the value of this book.

RICHARD T. ELY.

MADISON, WISCONSIN,
March, 1903.

LIST OF THE AUTHOR'S PUBLICATIONS

WHICH HAVE BEEN USED TO A GREATER OR LESS EXTENT IN THE PREPARATION OF THE PRESENT WORK

COMPETITION; ITS NATURE, ITS PERMANENCY, AND ITS BENEFI-CENCE. Address delivered as President of the American Economic Association, in Detroit, Michigan, Dec. 27, 1900. Printed in Publications of the American Economic Association, 1901.

MONOPOLIES AND TRUSTS. *International Journal of Ethics*, April, 1900.

AN ANALYSIS OF THE STEEL TRUST. *The Cosmopolitan*, August, 1901.

MUNICIPAL OWNERSHIP OF NATURAL MONOPOLIES. *North American Review*, March, 1901.

INHERITANCE OF PROPERTY. *North American Review*, July, 1891.

UNITED STATES INDUSTRIAL COMMISSION'S REPORT ON LABOR. *Yale Review*, November, 1902.

HOW TO AVERT STRIKES. *Boston Evening Transcript*, Aug. 3, 1901; also elsewhere.

INDUSTRIAL LIBERTY. Address delivered as President of the American Economic Association, Washington, D.C., Dec. 27, 1901. Printed in Publications of the American Economic Association, 1902.

REVIEW OF PROFESSOR J. MARK BALDWIN'S "SOCIAL AND ETHICAL INTERPRETATIONS." *The Expositor*, March, 1898.

OUR NEIGHBORS. Chapter VII, in "Social Law of Service." New York, 1896.

CONTENTS

xiii

CONTENTS

CONTENTS

CONTENTS

PART II

SOME SPECIAL PROBLEMS OF INDUSTRIAL EVOLUTION

CONTENTS

CONTENTS

PART I

GENERAL SURVEY

STUDIES IN THE EVOLUTION OF INDUSTRIAL SOCIETY

CHAPTER I

THE IDEA OF EVOLUTION IN SOCIETY

THE history of ideas is the history of man. Ideas distinguish man from all lower animals, and all that is significant in human history may be traced back to ideas. From time to time, in the history of mankind, an idea of such tremendous import has found acceptance in the minds and hearts of men that it has been followed by a new era in the progress of the human race. The idea of Jehovah, which found acceptance among the ancient Hebrews, was one of these germinal ideas, which made the world ever thereafter a different world. That idea has been moulding human history ever since it was first clearly received and promulgated. The idea of itself, from the time of its reception up to the present, has been growing larger, and more elevated and refined. It has undergone a perpetual process of purification, and has been one of the great psychical forces which give shape to human history. Christianity came into the world as the outcome of another grand idea, and since its reception the world has been a new world. Its mighty significance has been recognized in dating all events with reference to the founder of that religion. Everything which happens is either before Christ or after Christ. Altogether apart from any peculiar belief in the mission and person of Christ, this could not be otherwise. Passing on down the stream of human history, we come to still another idea which has made the world different from what it was before, and is thus giving direction to human history. This is the idea of evolution, the general acceptance of which we must recognize as the distinguishing characteristic of nineteenth century thought.

This idea of evolution is one of long growth.[1] Some foreshadowings may be found in the early philosophy of the Greeks, and the idea recurs from time to time in the history of philosophical speculation. By the time of Charles Darwin, many naturalists had become convinced in a general way that there was a development from the lower to the higher forms of life, but they had not been able to tell how it had taken place. The peculiar service of Darwin was the explanation of the method of biological development by means of the theory of natural selection. It was in 1859 that he published his great work entitled, "The Origin of Species by Means of Natural Selection,"

[1] For a history of the idea, see Osborn, "From the Greeks to Darwin," 2d ed., New York, 1899.

and so convincing was the evidence he submitted that the general acceptance of the idea of evolution dates from the publication of this book. It is interesting to note that both Darwin and Wallace, who discovered the theory of natural selection independently, received special assistance from Malthus' work on population.

Darwin's researches were restricted almost altogether to the evolution of the individual organism. Even now, when evolution is mentioned, we think of the evolution of the individual. It is from this standpoint that Huxley — Darwin's bulldog, as he was called — defines the term: " Evolution or development is, in fact, at present employed in biology as a general name for the history of the steps by which any living being has acquired the morphological and physiological characters which distinguish it."[1] A recent writer gives the following definition: " By evolution we mean to-day not only that all living forms have descended from those living in the past, but also that new forms have arisen from the old ones."[2] This writer says further that from the ranks of biologists few now arise to question the correctness of the theory of evolution, although many no longer regard Darwin's theory of natural selection as a sufficient

[1] "Evolution in Biology," 1878, Collected Essays, New York, 1896, Vol. II, p. 196.

[2] "Darwinism in the Light of Modern Criticism," by Thomas Hunt Morgan, Ph.D., Professor of Biology, Bryn Mawr College, *Harper's Monthly Magazine*, February, 1903, p. 476.

explanation of the method of development. The biologists, however, while confining themselves for the most part to the physiological and individual aspects of evolution, knew well enough that it had a wider meaning for man. To expound this wider and deeper meaning was the work of Herbert Spencer.

Four years before Darwin published his " Origin of Species," Spencer published his " Principles of Psychology," in which he enunciates the principle of mental evolution. Two years later (1857) he made a much wider application of the idea in an essay entitled, "Progress: Its Law and Cause." [1] The same process, he says in this essay, we may see " alike in the earliest changes of the Universe to which we can reason our way back ; and in the earliest changes which we can inductively establish; it is seen in the geologic and climatic evolution of the Earth, and of every single organism on its surface ; it is seen in the evolution of Humanity, whether contemplated in the civilized individual, or in the aggregation of races; it is seen in the evolution of Society in respect alike of its political, its religious, and its economical organization ; and it is seen in the evolution of all those endless concrete and abstract products of human activity which constitute the environment of our daily life." It is probably due to Herbert Spencer

[1] *Westminster Review*, April, 1857, p. 255. Reprinted in " Illustrations of Universal Progress; a Series of Discussions," by Herbert Spencer, New York, 1874.

more than to any other one person that we have come to recognize the applicability of evolution to the various departments of the social life of man. We have an evolution of the body, and also an evolution of the mind, and we have an evolution of society, which is the highest form of life.[1]

Evolution in its broadest terms is defined by Spencer as follows, " Evolution is an integration of matter and concomitant dissipation of motion ; during which the matter passes from an indefinite, incoherent homogeneity to a definite, coherent heterogeneity ; and during which the retained motion undergoes a parallel transformation." [2] This definition, although not exhaustive, is especially helpful as an approach to the study of the evolution of society.

Early society is little more than a mere mass of men, composed of individuals with like occupations, like habits, like beliefs. In a few individuals we see all. Even in physical characteristics, it is altogether probable that differences among highly civilized men are far more numerous. This is especially noticeable in the matter of color of hair

[1] For an interesting discussion of the relations of the individual man to society, see a paper by the late Professor Joseph Le Conte, entitled, " The Effects of the Theory of Evolution on Education," published in the Proceedings and Addresses of the Nationa. Educational Association, held in Denver, 1895, p. 149.

[2] " First Principles of a New System of Philosophy," 2d ed., New York, 1868, p. 396. See also an article by Spencer, entitled " What is Social Progress? " *Nineteenth Century Magazine*, Vol. XLIV, p. 348.

7

and eyes. Careful measurements of a large number of white and negro children have shown that
there is a greater diversity among white children
in all their normal physical characters.[1] Of
course, even the rudest society that we know is
not entirely homogeneous : there is a differentiation
on account of sex, age, and natural ability ; the
medicine men are different from the rest of the
tribe, and the various individuals are recognized
as belonging to different marriage groups ; and
yet, on the whole, one man lives about the same
life as does every other man.[2] In a hunting tribe,
all of the men are hunters and warriors. But
in a highly developed society, we find a vast and
growing number of groups, and within the groups
individuality becomes more marked. A military
life, a public life, a professional life, or a business or
industrial life, with its thousands of occupations, —
each puts its peculiar stamp on men, mentally and
physically.

This, however, is but a part of Spencer's definition. Along with this differentiation there is also

[1] Dr. A. Hrdlicka, in the *American Anthropologist*, Vol. XI,
p. 347.

[2] "The New Zealander . . . is acquainted with every department
of knowledge common to his race : he can build his house, can make
his canoe, his nets, his hooks and lines; he can manufacture snares
to suit every bird, and form his traps; he can fabricate his garments, and every tool and implement required. It is not a single
individual, or a few only, who are adepts in these various arts, but
all." — TAYLOR, "TE IKA A MAUI, or New Zealand and its Inhabitants," London, 2d ed., 1870, p. 3.

an integration, a binding together of the various groups. Early society is incoherent. When we read of a tribe [1] that has no home, nor hut, nor any fixed habitation, living only beneath the trees, and moving from place to place, according to the seasons and the search for wild fruits and roots, it is evident that the destruction of any part of the group would make no vital change in the life of the remainder. Not so in a developed society. Specialization has brought with it interdependence. Let the class that devotes itself to transportation, for example, cease working, and the disastrous and far-reaching consequences to the rest of the community can scarcely be imagined. Civilized society is coherent.

This view of the matter undoubtedly tells us something that is true about the development of society. We are convinced that there has been a social evolution, and that this has meant a growing complexity and coherence, and yet that does not reveal to us the causes that are at work. Neither Mr. Spencer nor any one else has been able to explain the actual process of social evolution in a way that has been generally accepted. Attempts have been made to carry over the principle of natural selection from biology into the study of the social life of man. Bagehot's "Physics and Politics,"

---

[1] "The Aborigines of the Province of Santa Marta, Columbia," *American Anthropologist* (New Series), Vol. III, p. 631, in an article bearing the above title, by Francis C. Nicholas, who gives a translation of part of a work written by a Spanish priest in 1739.

and Kidd's "Social Evolution" may be cited as illustrations. But before the method of social evolution is worked out satisfactorily, probably a good deal of further investigation will have to be carried on in the separate departments of social life.

Usually, when we speak of social evolution, we have in mind social progress, but it may also imply social degeneration. Just as an individual may degenerate into an idiot or a criminal, a whole people may sink into decay. The history of the ancient world is full of illustrations. But in many cases such a retrogression seems to be a part of a world progress. Greece and Rome decayed after their civilizations had borne fruit. Similarly, within each society, there is an atrophy of institutions no longer needed by the developing organism. A modern city has meant the decay of town meetings; the movement toward large scale production has meant the crushing out of many formerly flourishing enterprises.[1] But may not mankind as a whole degenerate? May not the human species finally arrive at old age and death? We who have faith in human nature will agree with Schäffle[2] that, although the physical conditions of the earth may so change as to make a high civilization impossible,

[1] See, on this point, "Evolution by Atrophy in Biology and Sociology," by Demoor and others, New York, 1899. (Translated from the French by Mrs. Chalmers Mitchell.)

[2] *Bau und Leben des socialen Körpers*, Tübingen, 1878, Vol. II, p. 445.

yet while physical conditions remain as they now are, a general human retrogression is not conceivable.

The life of man in society is a unit, but, on account of the limitations of the mind, it is necessary for purposes of study to divide it into parts, and to examine them separately. Thus, we have the social life spheres of literature, religion, politics, industry, etc. The work of those sciences which may be broadly classed as the humanities has in recent years largely consisted in tracing out the evolution in the separate departments of social life. Even ethics and religion are now conceived of as undergoing evolution both in theory and practice.[1] It is with the industrial life sphere that we are especially concerned.

[1] See article on "Evolution of Religion," in the "Dictionary of Philosophy and Psychology," edited by James Mark Baldwin, New York, 1902, where many references are given.

CHAPTER II

THE social organism, we have said, is a unit, but we may study it from various points of view in the same way that we may study the human body with special reference to the nervous system or the digestive system. The term "industrial society" is merely a short way of saying, "society viewed from the industrial standpoint." How much is included from this point of view? The tools and processes of production and the organization of industry at once occur to us. But in addition to these we must take into consideration the ways in which industry binds men together, forms them into classes, and how it affects their health and well-being. Then there are certain mental and moral characteristics that are of importance from this point of view, such as foresight, industry, honesty, and capacity for social coöperation; and finally, certain legal institutions, such as private property, inheritance, contract, and personal freedom, are the very corner-stones of our present economic life. The study of the industrial life sphere, therefore, is more than a study of machines and factories.

EVOLUTION AND INDUSTRIAL SOCIETY

Most people who think at all are well aware that changes have recently been going on in the economic world about them. The "trust" movement is so recent and so striking that it is observed by all. Yet this by no means implies a prevalence of the evolutionary point of view in the consideration of our industrial life. Very many look upon these changes as something to be deplored, as an abnormal condition, to be contrasted with a former long-continued period of independence and opportunity. The evolutionary point of view, on the contrary, emphasizes the fact that these present changes are merely a link in a great chain of continuous development that extends back to the beginning of human existence and that must continue in the future. The evolution of industrial society signifies a continuous change, a perpetual flux of economic relations and institutions. It is true, these changes do not always proceed with the same rapidity. They appear to be especially rapid just now, as they have been throughout the whole of the nineteenth century. It is, in fact, only within the last one hundred years that the industrial ties binding men together have become so extensive and intensive that the term "industrial society" has become familiar.

The improvements in the mechanical instruments of production are perhaps the most evident of the changes that constitute economic evolution. We need merely contrast the slow work of the mediæval copyists with the work of a modern press that is capable of printing and delivering, folded, twelve thousand twenty-four page papers per hour; or think first of the Iroquois woman, tilling the soil with the shoulder blade of a deer, and then think of a modern steam plough; or compare the simple loom of the Pueblo woman with the complex machinery of a modern cotton factory; or again, compare the human carriers employed by the ancient Mexican merchants, transporting [1] fifty pounds each five or six leagues a day, with the long line of cars in a modern freight train. How recent in the world's history these improvements in technical processes really are, is strikingly illustrated by the following diagram : [2] —

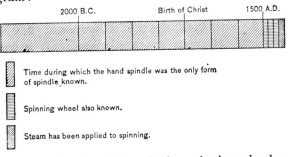

2000 B.C.   Birth of Christ   1500 A.D.

Time during which the hand spindle was the only form of spindle known.

Spinning wheel also known.

Steam has been applied to spinning.

We ordinarily think of the spinning-wheel as something very old and primitive, yet the period

[1] "The Despatches of Hernando Cortes," translated from the Spanish by George Folsom, New York and London, 1843, p. 113; also Prescott, "History of the Conquest of Mexico," New York, 1854, Vol. I, p. 348.

[2] From the First Report of the Labor Museum at Hull House, Chicago, 1901–1902, p. 9.

during which it has been used is but a small fraction of the time in which man depended on the hand spindle. We are told[1] that many of the Italian women who come to Chicago have never seen spinning-wheels, and look upon them as a new and wonderful invention. The period during which steam has been applied to cotton manufacture is even still shorter (since 1785).

An increasing division of labor and of occupations has accompanied these technical improvements. Long ago Adam Smith pointed out that what is the work of one man in a rude state of society is generally the work of several in an improved one.[2] The degree to which this process is being carried is strikingly illustrated by the growth in the actual number of occupations which people pursue for a living. A Boston directory for 1789 gives less than two hundred occupations; at the present time there are probably as many as ten thousand.[3] This will not seem at all incredible when we consider the extent of the present

[1] From the First Report of the Labor Museum at Hull House, Chicago, 1901–1902, p. 9.

[2] It happens, however, that in the particular illustration that he chose, the number of occupations has recently been growing less. In the making of pins there were seventeen operations by the hand method, and now by the machine method there are only ten. (Thirteenth Annual Report of the United States Commissioner of Labor, 1898, Vol. I, p. 63.)

[3] Judging from the German census of occupations (see Bücher's "Industrial Evolution," translated by S. M. Wickett, New York, 1901, p. 324). Our own census of 1900 gives only 303 groups of occupations, which is less than the number given in the census of 1870.

subdivision of one particular occupation of the earlier period. Instead of one or two men performing all the operations in the making of a boot, we have to-day a front cutter, back cutter, back stay cutter, top cutter, facing cutter, lining cutter, sorter and buncher, size and case marker, stay skiver, top skiver, crimper, front trimmer, top front stitcher, top back stitcher, and so on to as many as one hundred and thirteen.[1] The making of a hand rake is divided among sawyers, turners, tenoners, truckmen, straighteners, binders, borers, sanders, planers, moulders, trimmers, finishers, etc.[2]

Illustrations of the division of occupations can be given from their own experience by many persons now living. The writer recalls a man who was at the same time doctor, preacher, and farmer, and another who was a farmer, shoemaker, and carpenter. De Tocqueville, who visited the United States in 1831, says that almost all the farmers combined some trade with agriculture.[3] Schoolteacher and surgeon is a combination found in early Boston, and in England it was at one time customary for barbers to be also surgeons.[4]

Not only has there been a constant tendency to

[1] Thirteenth Annual Report of the United States Commissioner of Labor, 1898, Vol. II, p. 529.   [2] *Ibid.*, p. 483.

[3] "Democracy in America," translated by Henry Reeve, 5th ed., Boston, 1873, Vol. II, p. 191.

[4] A survival is found in the colors of the barber's pole, the red indicating blood-letting. In Baltimore, doubtless as elsewhere in the United States, to this day one can find a barber advertising "cupping and bleeding."

divide the work of one man among several, but entirely new occupations have been springing up. Here are a few of those that do not appear in the Boston directory for 1789: stenographer, iceman, life insurance agent, photographer, letter-carrier, advertisement writer, expert accountant, bicycle repairer, funeral director, commercial traveller, elevator tender, window-dresser, lithographer, stereotyper, and in addition there are a host of occupations that are suggested by the mere mention of the words steam and electricity.

Such changes as the foregoing imply also a changing economic organization. The great enterprises in every line of business are carried on largely by corporations, and this seems to us very natural; yet in 1776 Adam Smith could write: "The only trades which it seems possible for a joint stock company to carry on successfully, without an exclusive privilege, are those of which all the operations are capable of being reduced to what is called a routine, or to such a uniformity of method which admits of little or no variation. Of this kind is, first, the banking trade; secondly, the trade of insurance from fire, and from sea risk and capture in time of war; thirdly, the trade of making and maintaining a navigable cut or canal; and fourthly, the similar trade of bringing water for the supply of a great city." [1] The typical manufacturing establishment a hundred years ago was a little shop where a master mechanic

[1] "Wealth of Nations," Bk. V, Ch. I, Pt. III, Art. I.

worked with hand tools, aided perhaps by two or three journeymen and apprentices. Now it is a large plant, using natural forces as motive power. It is owned by a vast industrial corporation, and over against the capital which owns and directs the establishment, we have hundreds and even thousands of men working with tools which they do not own. Those connected with a modern railway form a vast hierarchy of stockholders, officers, clerks, station agents, enginemen, firemen, conductors, brakemen, machinists, carpenters, shopmen, switchmen, flagmen, watchmen, telegraphers, all closely organized. The ties binding them to the rest of the community are so close that the cessation of their operations must mean the keenest distress, even death, to thousands and hundreds of thousands. Such a development has brought with it widely separated classes, the common laborer marking one extreme, the railway magnate the other, the one living in a shanty, the other in a palace, and both probably never knowing each other. At Chicago Commons (a social settlement at Grand Avenue and Morgan Streets, Chicago) recently " an employer and an employee who had sustained that relationship for seventeen years met for the first time." [1]

The banks which we now see in any American city mean that the industrial world in which we

---

[1] "The Labor Contract" (Ms., p. 74), August, 1902, a thesis submitted to the University of Wisconsin for the degree of Doctor of Philosophy, by Dr. Margaret A. Schaffner.

live is a different one from that familiar to the
fathers of this republic. A little more than a hundred years ago there were but three banks in the
United States. Now there are more than two
thousand times that number. Had all the banks
of 1790 failed, it is safe to say that three-fourths
of all the people of the United States would not
have known the difference. Should all these
banks fail to-day, there is scarcely a man or woman
in the United States who would not feel the disastrous effects, and words could not describe the suffering which would ensue, not only to the people of
the United States, but to the entire world. The
banking institutions of to-day mean a new economic
world, a world bound together by the closest ties.

New words in our vocabulary and the changed
meanings of old ones afford further illustrations.
The word "manufacturing" is used by Adam
Smith to mean working with one's hands, and he
says that a man may become rich by employing
a multitude of manufacturers. We call a maiden
a spinster because it was taken for granted that
the unmarried daughters of a family should largely
occupy themselves with the spinning-wheel. A
furlong meant originally a "furrow long," and reminds us of the early English manor where the
common fields were ploughed in acre pieces (or
less), the furrow on one side being forty rods in
length.[1] The word "farmer" refers to the mediæval English tenant who held a piece of land for

[1] Cheney, " Industrial and Social History of England," p. 34.

which he paid the lord "a 'farm' or *firma*, that is, a settled established sum, in place of the various forms of profit that might have been secured from it by the lord of the manor." [1] Our common word "staple" meant an established market, and in early England certain towns were designated as ones to which all goods had to be brought before being exported. These were "staple towns," and the principal commodities exported (wool, skins, and leather) became known as staple commodities. The fact that the German traders who came to England in the Middle Ages were called Easterlings accounts for the use of the word "sterling" in connection with English money. Such expressions as socialist, scab, government by injunction, walking delegate, collective bargaining, sliding scale, watered stock, wheat pit, workingmen's insurance, factory legislation, bonanza farming, captain of industry, full dinner pail, coöperation and profit-sharing, municipal ownership, mail order business, etc., are mostly terms which George Washington would not have understood at all.

Such considerations as the foregoing impress us with the fact that the economic world is a changing world. But are the changes which we have been considering, ordered changes? Does law underlie them? The universality of the reign of law is a fundamental hypothesis of modern science, and unless we think things happen by chance, we must affirm that there is order in the changes in

[1] Cheney, "Industrial and Social History of England," p. 129.

the industrial world, as there is order in the natural universe.

The idea of the evolution of society in general has been one of slow, general acceptance, and perhaps still more slowly has been received the idea of the evolution of industrial society, with all the implications which necessarily follow from this idea. Nevertheless, the idea of the evolution of industrial society was clearly advanced more than fifty years ago, several years prior to the publication of Herbert Spencer's "Psychology," by the group of German economists who are now ordinarily designated as the German Historical School. Of these, the three most prominent were Bruno Hildebrand, Wilhelm Roscher, and Karl Knies, — the last-named of whom was the honored and revered professor under whom it was the author's privilege to study as a student in Heidelberg. Even before their time Friedrich List, a German economist, who had lived for several years in the United States and was deeply impressed with our growth, had advanced the idea of an industrial evolution. In his " National System of Political Economy," he says, " In the economical development of nations, it is necessary to distinguish the following principal stages : the savage state, the pastoral state, the agricultural state, the agricultural and manufacturing state, and finally, the agricultural, manufacturing, and commercial state." [1] He was interested

[1] Translation from the German by G. A. Matile, Philadelphia, 1856, p. 72.

especially in the problem of the protective tariff, holding that the policy which was suitable for one period in a nation's growth could not be safely followed in a subsequent period. In other words, he taught clearly that no one could properly describe himself in absolute terms either as a free-trader or a protectionist, but that a man might be rationally a free-trader at one period of development, a protectionist at a later period, and again, at a subsequent period, like that now attained by the United States, a free-trader. So, a man could be a free-trader in one country, as England, and a protectionist in another country, as Germany or the United States in his day. This is simply adduced as an illustration. The historical economists must have received valuable suggestions from List, but they were most of all influenced by the comparative and historical school of jurisprudence, so ably led by that great jurist, Savigny. The relativity of human institutions was the central thought, and the only one which need concern us at the present time. They protested against what was called absolutism and perpetualism, absolutism meaning that one policy could be a good policy for all countries, and perpetualism, that one policy could be good for all periods of time.

In 1848 Karl Marx and his friend, Friedrich Engels, presented to the world a theory of evolution which is called by its adherents scientific socialism. The basis of that theory is the proposition that in every historical epoch the social, political, and intellectual life is determined by prevailing economic conditions, and that in the future, the economic conditions will be such as to necessitate inevitably a socialistic organization of society. To this we shall recur in a later chapter. The followers of Marx rank him with Darwin and Spencer as an evolutionary thinker.[1]

In 1896 Herbert Spencer published the third volume of his "Principles of Sociology," in which he traces the development of industrial institutions in particular. It did not receive very much attention because the main ideas which it contains, such as the growth of specialization and integration, the distinction between the militant and industrial types of society, and the author's uncompromising hostility to socialism, had been made familiar by his earlier writings.

Investigation has, perhaps, not proceeded far enough to enable us to state with great positiveness what the laws of change are. We have, indeed, in this investigation one of the richest fields for the cultivation of science. These changes are in part psychical in their causes, and we do not yet know enough about the laws of the individual mind or of the social mind to enable us to know what we should like about the order of industrial evolution.

[1] In recent years a high position among the world's thinkers has been attributed to Marx even by non-socialists. Professor E. R. A. Seligman of Columbia University may be mentioned in this connection, and the reader is referred to his work, "The Economic Interpretation of History."

Nevertheless, the various classifications of the stages of industrial evolution that have been proposed are not without value. The one suggested by List has been usually followed in the past, so far as its main outline is concerned, and it seems to the writer that, in spite of all criticism, it is still, with some modifications, the most serviceable as a framework within which to study the course of economic development, and accordingly we shall follow it as a basis for our classification in the next chapter. As will be shown, however, it is not contradictory to the other classifications that have been proposed.

CHAPTER III

I. *Introductory*

THE way in which people get their living is in very intimate relation with their whole social life. It is probable, says Morgan, "that the great epochs of human progress have been identified, more or less directly, with the enlargement of the sources of subsistence."[1] When men rely on hunting and fishing for a living, they are very different men from what they are when they have settled down to a predominantly agricultural life, or when they satisfy their wants by the aid of vast aggregations of capital.[2]

---

[1] Morgan, "Ancient Society," New York, 1878, p. 19.

[2] Karl Marx and his followers exaggerate greatly the influence of the economic life of a people upon their social life in general, holding what is known as the materialistic conception of history, or, as Professor Edwin R. A. Seligman calls it, the economic interpretation of history. This doctrine is defined by Professor Seligman as follows: " We understand, then, by the theory of the economic interpretation of history, not that all history is to be explained in economic terms alone, but that the chief considerations in human progress are the social considerations, and that the important factor in the social change is the economic factor. The economic interpretation of history means, not that the economic relations exert an exclusive influence, but that they exert a preponderant influence in shaping the progress of society."— The Economic Interpretation

The ways of getting a living, therefore, ought to be a serviceable point of view from which to study the development of man, and from this point of view we get the following stages:—

1. The hunting and fishing stage.
2. The pastoral stage.
3. The agricultural stage.
4. The handicraft stage.
5. The industrial stage.

> 1st phase: Universal competition as an ideal.
>
> 2d phase: Concentration.
>
> 3d phase: Integration.

II. *The Hunting and Fishing Stage*

If we accept the doctrine of evolution, we must be able to look back upon a time when our ancestors were living a mere animal existence. This indeed requires no great stretch of the imagina-

of History," *Political Science Quarterly*, March, 1902, Vol. XVII, p. 76.

When stated in this mild form, it is difficult to see why the doctrine should have aroused so much discussion. The controversy seems simply to be whether we shall say the economic factor is *the* most or *a* most important factor. But to the Marxists generally the materialistic conception of history signifies far more than this. For example, one of them recently stated that religion is not a cause, but a product, that is, of economic life. See "The Economic Interpretation of History," by Mrs. May Wood Simons, in the *International Socialist Review*, March, 1903. This subject receives further treatment from a somewhat different viewpoint in the chapter on the "Widening and Deepening Range of Ethical Obligation," Pt. II, Ch. XII.

tion when one has read descriptions of some of the most primitive tribes upon the earth to-day,[1] although, to be sure, there is a great gap between the lowest of them and the highest of the animals. The Negritos of the Philippines, the Veddahs of Ceylon, the Fuegians of South America, and the Australian aborigines afford illustrations.

Take, for example, some of the tribes of central Australia. They are described as wandering about in small groups of one or two families, camping at favorite spots where the food is abundant. There is no such thing as a chief of the tribe. In their ordinary condition they are almost completely naked, for the idea of making any kind of clothing as a protection against the cold does not seem to have entered their minds, notwithstanding the fact that the temperature at times falls below the freezing point. Their habitation is merely a rough covering of shrubs for protection against the wind. Time is no object to them, and if there be no lack of food, the men and women lounge about while the children laugh and play. When they are hungry, the women, armed with digging sticks and *pitchis* (wooden troughs for carrying food), search for liz-

---

[1] Darwin, on first seeing the Fuegians, wrote: " It was without exception the most curious and interesting spectacle I ever beheld : I could not have believed how wide was the difference between savage and civilized man : it is greater than between a wild and domesticated animal, inasmuch as in man there is a greater power of improvement." — " Journal of Researches into the Natural History and Geology of the Countries visited during the Voyage of H. M. S. *Beagle* around the World," New York, 1873, p. 205.

ards and small marsupials, while the men look for larger game. Everything that is edible is used for food, the honey-ants being a favorite dish. They know the use of fire, but they have little in the way of implements besides the spear, shield, spear-thrower, boomerang, stone knives, and, rarely, hatchets. When times are prosperous they are light-hearted; but there is always an undercurrent of anxious feeling which may assert itself, and then they think of some hostile medicine man who may be trying to harm them with his evil magic. They decorate their bodies with scars, and observe a strict code of custom and ceremony. If a man's ancestor painted a white line across his forehead in the performance of a certain ceremony, for example, that line he must also paint.[1]

The North American Indians offer especially good material for studying the hunting and fishing stage because of their varying degrees of development within that stage. In the northern and western part of the continent we find purely hunting tribes that did not cultivate the soil; in the eastern half of what is now the United States a simple kind of soil cultivation was generally practised; and the village Indians of New Mexico, Mexico, and Central America depended almost exclusively upon the produce of their fields for sub-

[1] This description is taken from Spencer and Gillen's "The Native Tribes of Central Australia," London, 1899, Ch. I, *passim.*

sistence, used irrigation, and built houses usually more than one story high.[1]

This last group of tribes, indeed, might be put in the agricultural stage, although they did not use domesticated animals in tilling the soil. Confining our attention, then, to the first two groups, let us ask what are the characteristics of man in this first stage of economic development.

The life of primitive man is nomadic. An early writer says, "From the first land (which is Newfoundland) to the country of the Armouchiquois, a distance of nearly three hundred leagues, the people are nomads, without agriculture, never stopping longer than five or six weeks in a place."[2] And another: "They (the Sioux) live on wild oats . . . and by hunting. . . . They have no fixed Abode, but travel in great Companies like the *Tartars*, and never stay in one Place longer than the Chace detains them."[3] Such a wandering life is plainly necessary so long as people depend on what they can find for a living. This characteristic applies to a less extent to the more advanced tribes of the East and South,[4] who

[1] Morgan, "Houses and House Life of the American Aborigines," United States Geographical and Geological Survey, "Contributions to North American Ethnology," Vol. IV, p. 42.

[2] Lescarbot, "La Conversion des Savvages, 1610," in "The Jesuit Relations and Allied Documents," edited by Reuben Gold Thwaites, 73 vols., Cleveland, 1896–1901, Vol. I, p. 83.

[3] Charlevoix, "Voyage to Canada," London, 1763, p. 110.

[4] Jones, "Antiquities of the Southern Indians," New York, 1873, p. 297.

had learned to cultivate the soil.[1]   The Indians of Pennsylvania, for example, raised maize, potatoes, beans, pumpkins, squashes, cucumbers, melons, and occasionally cabbages and turnips.[2]

The method of soil cultivation forms another characteristic of this stage.   It has been aptly termed "hoe culture."   The work was done by hand with the aid of sticks and rude hoes and spades made of bones, shells, or stone.[3]   In a Southern tribe the men broke up the surface of the ground with fish bones attached to wooden handles, and after them came the women, who, with the aid of sticks, made holes into which they dropped the beans or grains of corn which they carried in small baskets.[4]   Ploughs and draught animals were not used.   The field labor was done chiefly by the women,[5] although the men occasionally helped.   In fact, one writer says that the

[1] The extent to which the Indians relied on the products of their fields for subsistence is a matter of some doubt.   In some cases it may have been the chief source (Jones, *loc. cit.*, p. 308), but not as a rule.   The best general reference on the subject is "The Mounds of the Mississippi Valley," by Lucien Carr, Annual Report of the Board of Regents of the Smithsonian Institution, 1891, Vol. I, pp. 507 ff.

[2] Heckewelder, "An Account of the History, Manners, and Customs of the Indian Nations, who once inhabited Pennsylvania and the Neighboring States."   Published in Transactions of American Philosophical Society, Philadelphia, 1819, Vol. I, p. 184.

[3] Abbott, "Primitive Industry," Salem, Mass., 1881, Ch. XVI.

[4] Jones, "Antiquities of the Southern Indians," p. 301.

[5] Hugh Jones, "Present State of Virginia," 1724, reprinted, New York, 1865, p. 9.

Iroquois are the only tribe among whom it cannot be shown that the warriors did take some part either in clearing the ground or in cultivating the crop.[1] To illustrate the fact that the women were the toilers while the men devoted their attention to hunting and fighting, it is not necessary to go to the accounts of early travellers. The same division may be seen among the Indians on their reservations. The woman's work in a Colorado reservation is thus described : " Each day, as the sun descends, she and her daughters come into the village from the timber valleys loaded with firewood — the load weighing from twenty to one hundred pounds ; she rises first in the morning, and builds the fire and prepares the breakfast . . .; as soon as this is over she is out in the sun stretching or dressing buckskin or buffalo hides, or stroking down beaver or otter skins, or cutting out garments, or sewing or ornamenting them with bead work or embroidery, often in a neat, artistic manner, with symmetrically flowing lines; and, except in rare cases, she has no idle hours. The truth is, an Indian village is, so far as the women are concerned, as full of active industry as any factory village of New England. Meanwhile the men have nothing to do." [2]

[1] Carr, *loc. cit*, p. 511. See also "The Jesuit Relations and Allied Documents," Vol. LXV, p. 133.

[2] N. C. Meeker, in the Greeley (Colo.) *Tribune*, December 11, 1878, quoted in Boyd's "History of Greeley and the Union Colony of Colorado," Greeley, 1890, p. 328.

In an unsettled life, where labor in the fields forms but a minor part, if any, of the food-getting activities, there is not much opportunity for the development of the institution of slavery. There was little incentive to refrain from killing the captives taken in battle, and when the lives of the prisoners were spared, it was very common for them to be adopted as members of the tribe. Speaking of the captives, one writer says, " Many are killed, but if one outlives this trial, he is adopted into a family as a son, and treated with paternal kindness; and if he avoids their suspicions of going away, is allowed the same privileges as their own people." [1] Heckewelder says, " The prisoners are generally adopted by the families of their conquerors in the place of lost or deceased relations or friends, where they soon become domesticated and are so kindly treated that they never wish themselves away again." [2] On the other hand, slaves were held to some extent and compelled to work. Of certain Canadian tribes, La Hontan says, " The Women Slaves are employed to Sow and Reap the *Indian-Corn;* and the Men Slaves have for their Business the Hunting and Shooting where there is any Fatigue, tho' their Masters will very often help them." [3] One

---

[1] Filson, " The Discovery, Settlement, and Present State of Kentucky," New York, 1793, p. 102.

[2] *Loc. cit.*, p. 211.

[3] La Hontan, " New Voyages to North America," London, 1703, Vol. II, p. 18.

of the early Jesuits [1] speaks of three classes of slaves among the Iroquois; and General Ely S. Parker,[2] himself an educated Iroquois, says the captives helped the women.

Let us turn now to the mental and moral characteristics of people in this stage, so far as they have an economic bearing. Professor Franklin H. Giddings [3] has called attention to their unbusiness-like way of doing things, and certainly one cannot read the constant references by missionaries and travellers to the large part that magic and ceremony played in their lives, without agreeing that this is a most prominent characteristic. Charlevoix gives the following instance: "When a Bear is killed, the Hunter puts the End of his lighted Pipe between his Teeth, blows into the Bowl; and thus filling the Mouth and Throat of the Beast with Smoak, he conjures its Spirit to bear no Malice for what he has just done to the Body, and not to oppose him in his future Huntings." [4] In September the Karoks have a great dance to propitiate the spirits of the earth and the forest in order to prevent disastrous land-slides, forest fires, earthquakes, drought, and other calamities.[5] The Ojibway Indians, in

[1] "The Jesuit Relations and Allied Documents," Vol. XLIII, p. 293.   [2] In a letter quoted by Carr, *loc cit.*

[3] *The Political Science Quarterly*, in an article entitled, "The Economic Ages," June, 1901, Vol. XVI, p. 202.

[4] "Voyage to Canada," p. 57.

[5] Powers, "The Tribes of California," United States Geographical and Geological Survey, "Contributions to North American Ethnology," Vol. III, p. 28.

Canada, make a feast before commencing to gather the rice, and none are allowed to gather the grain until after it.[1] The Dakotas set apart the first corn or wild rice of the season, and the first duck or goose killed when they appear in the spring, for a holy feast, at which those Indians only who are entitled to wear the badge of having slain an enemy are invited.[2] Lumholtz[3] found a village of Mexican Indians having twenty-five shamans or priest-doctors for only 180 households. Loskiel[4] says that before an Indian sets out for a long hunt, he usually shoots one or more deer and keeps a feast of sacrifice, inviting the old men to assist him in praying for success. If he shoots nothing for several days, he swallows a small dose of a preparation made by the old men who are no longer able to hunt. Father Le Petit says of the Natchez: "They never plant their fields without having first presented the seed in the temple with the accustomed ceremonies."[5]

Another prominent characteristic is their childish lack of forethought. A missionary among the Ojibways[6] says that from January to March is

[1] Jenks, "Wild Rice Gatherers of the Upper Lakes," p. 1091. Reprinted from Nineteenth Annual Report of the Bureau of Ethnology.   [2] *Ibid.*

[3] Lumholtz, "Unknown Mexico," New York, 1902, p. 312.

[4] Loskiel, "History of the Missions of the United Brethren among the Indians in North America," translated from the German, London, 1794, p. 76.

[5] "The Jesuit Relations and Allied Documents," Vol. LXVIII, p. 139.   [6] Minnesota Historical Society Collections, Vol. IX, p. 72.

their starving time, although a very few days' labor would have raised all the corn and potatoes they could use. Often when suffering severely from hunger in the dead of winter, they bitterly lament their own improvidence, and vow that if they live till spring they will do differently. But when the abundance of summer comes the starving of the past winter is forgotten; the time is passed in dancing and pleasure, with no thought for the future and no provision made for it. All the Indians who are middle-aged recall the severe starvation to which when young they were peri- odically subjected, and through which they hardly lived. Loskiel says the Iroquois preserved their crops in round holes dug in the earth at some dis- tance from the houses, lined and covered with dry leaves or grass; but if the winter happened to be severe, and the snow prevented them from hunting, a general famine ensued, by which many died.[1] An Apache woman at one of the military posts in eastern Arizona, on receiving her rations for the week, consumed all of them at a sitting, trusting to her ability to find sufficient food to sustain her until next ration day.[2] "I told them that they did not manage well," says Father Le Jeune, of the Cana- dian Indians, "and that it would be better to reserve these feasts for future days, and in doing this they would not be so pressed with hunger. They laughed

[1] *Loc. cit.*, p. 68.
[2] Hoffman, "The Menomini Indians," Fourteenth Annual Re- port Bureau of Ethnology, Pt. I, p. 287.

at me. 'To-morrow (they said) we shall make another feast with what we shall capture.' Yes, but more often they captured only cold and wind."[1] Of course, thought for the future was not entirely lacking. The more advanced tribes had made evident progress in this direction. The Indians of North Carolina had corn-cribs,[2] and the villages of the Cherokees are said to have abounded with "hogs, poultry, and every thing sufficient for the support of a reasonable life."[3] But man's forethought had to undergo a tremendous development before a modern civilized life was possible. To this we shall recur again.

Another thing that we must notice about this early stage is communal life. There were no starving poor among them, unless they all were starving. "Every citizen," says Bartram,[4] "has free access to the public granary when his own private stores are consumed." Private property in land was not thought of, although possibly a slight beginning in this direction may be seen in the separation of the patch cultivated by one family from the next adjacent one by a strip of grass or other boundary.[5] Articles of personal

[1] "The Jesuit Relations," Vol. VI, p. 283.

[2] Lawson, "History of North Carolina (1714)," Raleigh, 1860, p. 35.

[3] Adair, "History of the North American Indians," London 1775, p. 230.

[4] "Travels through North and South Carolina, etc.," Philadelphia, 1791, p. 512, and La Hontan, *loc. cit.*, Vol. II, p. 7.

[5] Bartram, p. 512.

use were, however, recognized as belonging to their users. This does not necessarily indicate a conception of ownership such as ours, but the things were looked upon as a part of the personality of the user.[1] "They are accustomed," one writer remarks, "to take everything that belongs to the deceased, skins, bow, utensils, wigwams, etc., and burn them all, howling and shouting certain cries, sorceries, and invocations to the evil spirit."[2] Living in common has often appealed to people as something unselfish, and a condition to which we should, if possible, return. But whatever the future may make possible, whether or not a man might some day, as John Stuart Mill suggests, dig and weave for his country as eagerly as he fights for it, it is clear that in this early stage some powerful incentive was necessary to encourage men to labor steadily and take thought for the future. That incentive was to be furnished above all by the institution of private property.

When people live on what they find, as in the purely hunting stage, there is little occasion for the development of trade. On the contrary, war with the surrounding tribes is the rule. The development of commerce and the diminishing frequency of war have steadily accompanied an advancing civilization. It is interesting to note, in passing, the close connection between gift-giving

[1] See Veblen, "The Beginnings of Ownership," *American Journal of Sociology*, November, 1898.

[2] "The Jesuit Relations and Allied Documents," Vol. I, p. 169.

and trade among the American Indians. To accept a present was to bind oneself to return an equivalent. A missionary among the Canadian Indians says they brought him some elk meat, and knowing that they expected a present also, he asked what they wanted. They desired wine and gunpowder, but when they found they could not get it, they carried back their meat.[1] This seems to be general among primitive people.

What has been said about hunting tribes applies in the main to those who derive their main sustenance from fishing. Fishing may have been an earlier occupation of mankind than hunting, but it offers greater possibilities for development when the tribe lives near the seacoast. A more stationary and less warlike life is possible, because the food supply is not so easily exhausted in one place, and there is great opportunity for the development of skill in fashioning contrivances for catching fish. The inhabitants of the South Sea Islands made salmon nets " forty fathoms long and twelve or more feet deep."[2] When a chief desired to make such a net, he called upon the other chiefs for assistance, — an instance of the development of social coöperation.

So long as man depends upon what Nature furnishes of her own accord, he does not make

[1] "The Jesuit Relations and Allied Documents," Vol. VI, pp. 7 and 257.

[2] Ellis, "Polynesian Researches," 2d ed., London, 1831, Vol. I, pp. 140 ff.

much progress. It is only when he learns to want
many things and to labor steadily that she gives up
her treasures. He had to learn, also, to coöperate
with the members of other tribes instead of trying
to kill them.

III. *The Pastoral Stage*

A great step in advance was made by man when
he learned to utilize domesticated animals for food
and work. He seems first to have tamed animals
for amusement. An early traveller says : " There
are few Villages in france where there are more hens
and Cocks than in that of the houmas [a Choctaw
tribe] because they never kill any, and will not
even eat any of those that their Dogs quite often
kill. When one wishes to obtain chickens from
them, He must not say that he intends to kill or
eat them." [1] Cortés says there were in Mexico
three hundred men whose sole employment it was
to take care of the emperor's pet birds.[2] In Africa
we find the Ovambo, "very rich in cattle and fond
of animal diet, yet their beasts would seem to be
kept for show rather than for food." [3]

The American natives did not reach the pastoral
stage from their own development. In South
America the llama and alpaca were domesticated,

[1] "Gravier's Voyage," 1700, "Jesuit Relations and Allied Documents," Vol. LXV, p. 151.

[2] "Despatches of Hernando Cortes," translated by George Folsom, p. 122.

[3] Anderson, " Four Years in the Wilds of Africa," Philadelphia, 1856, p. 153.

while nearly all the Indians had dogs, and Major
J. W. Powell thinks that in time they would have
learned to domesticate the bison.[1] Since the arrival
of the whites, the Navajo Indians in northeastern
Arizona have become a pastoral people. One
observer[2] describes them as follows : " The region
is especially adapted for sheep culture, and the
Navajo equally well adapted for shepherds, coin-
ciding circumstances which have happily influenced
their destiny, transforming them wholly into a
peaceable, pastoral tribe. Every family is possessed of a flock of sheep and goats and a band
of horses. . . . To maintain the flocks in sufficient pasture, they move them to different grazing
grounds, at least twice a year. . . . Vivid traditions are still extant of those early times before the
Spaniard brought sheep and horses to their land,
when they lived on the spoil of the chase, on wild
fruits, grass seeds, and piñon nuts. Indian corn,
however, was known to them apparently from the
earliest times, but while they remained a mere
hunting tribe, they detested the labor of planting.
But as their numbers increased, the game, more
regularly hunted, became scarce, and to maintain
themselves in food, necessity forced them to a
more general cultivation of corn, and the regular

[1] In his article on the American Indians, in " The United States
of America," edited by N. S. Shaler, New York, 1894, Vol. I, p. 251;
but Professor Shaler (" Domesticated Animals," New York, 1895,
p. 106) says the bison seems to be essentially undomesticable.

[2] A. M. Stephen, "The Navajo," *American Anthropologist*,
Vol. VI, p. 347.

practice of planting became established among them."

The Todas of India, who live chiefly from their herds of buffaloes, have a tradition of a time when they subsisted on roots.[1] "The move upward from the life of the hunter to that of the herdsman," says Tylor, "is well seen in the far North, the home of the reindeer. Among the Esquimaux, the reindeer was only hunted. But Siberian tribes not only hunted them wild, but tamed them."[2] For further illustrations of existing pastoral peoples, we may mention the nomads of central Asia and some of the Arabian and other African tribes.

It is not intended to assert here that all peoples have once been pastoral nomads. Such a life depends in large measure upon physiographic conditions. The steppes of central Asia, with their extremes of temperature, offering pasturage during but a part of the summer, and becoming an inhospitable desert at another, are peculiarly suited to nomadic pastoral life. Similarly, in part of the arid belt of the United States, cattle-raising is almost the sole occupation.[3] It may well be that the first cattle were domesticated by peoples that had already learned to carry on hoe culture [4] in permanent villages, so that these never became pastoral nomads, deriving their main subsistence

[1] Marshall, "Travels amongst the Todas," London, 1873, p. 82.

[2] "Anthropology," New York, 1891, p. 219.

[3] Roosevelt, "Ranch Life and the Hunting Trail," New York, 1899, p. 1.   [4] See *ante*, p. 30.

from their animals,[1] but inasmuch as we can trace
back the history of many civilized peoples[2] to a
time when cattle-raising was their chief occupation,
it does not seem improper to make the pastoral life
a separate stage in human development.   It typi-
fies a great human achievement.   It is in those
regions in which an agricultural life presents
special difficulties that an arrested development
has preserved for us in some measure a record of
the influence of that change.   In our own history
we have an epitome of the world's experience in
this respect.   In the words of Professor F. J.
Turner, " The United States lies like a huge page
in the history of society.   Line by line, as we read
this continental page from west to east, we find the
record of social evolution.   It begins with the
Indian and the hunter; it goes on to tell of the disintegration of savagery by the entrance of the
trader, the pathfinder of civilization.   We read
the annals of the pastoral stage in ranch life; the
exploitation of the soil by the raising of unrotated
crops of corn and wheat in sparsely settled farming
communities; the intensive culture of the denser
farm settlements; and finally, the manufacturing
organization with city and factory system." [3]   That
is, the cattle-raising frontier has given away con-

[1] Cf. Schmoller, "Grundriss der allgemeinen Volkswirtschaftslehre," Leipzig, 1900, pp. 195 and 196.

[2] See below, pp. 43-45.

[3] "The Significance of the Frontier in American History,"
Annual Report of the American Historical Association for 1893,
Washington, 1894, p. 207.

tinually to higher stages, except in the regions where for a time, or permanently, agriculture has not been possible, namely, in the arid belt.

In this second stage man relies less directly upon nature for his food. He learns to take more thought for the future. His herds and flocks represent a body of social capital which must be preserved intact, and of which the increase only can be used. There is a development of the institution of private property, not as yet in land, but in movable wealth, and in consequence we are not surprised to find the contrast between rich and poor making its appearance. Among the Kirghiz of central Asia only the rich have more than one wife.[1] A murder is paid for with six hundred head of cattle. Borrowing at interest and rules concerning the inheritance of property make their appearance.[2] Warlike habits continue; the men, although extremely lazy and slovenly, are brave and capable of undergoing great hardship. There is no special development of the arts nor of slavery, for these are especially characteristic of a relatively peaceful existence.

IV. *The Agricultural Stage*

The change from the pastoral to the agricultural stage may be exemplified from the history of the Jews. In Genesis we read: "And Abram was

---

[1] Moser, "Durch Central-Asien," Ch. II, Leipzig, 1888.

[2] Lansdell, "Russian Central Asia," Boston, 1885, Vol. I, Chs. XXII and XXIII.

very rich in cattle, in silver, and in gold. . . . And Lot also, which went with Abram, had flocks, and herds, and tents. . . . And Abram said unto Lot, Let there be no strife, I pray thee, between me and thee, and between my herdmen and thy herdmen; for we be brethren." But in Samuel the agricultural stage is suggested: "And he will appoint him captains over thousands and captains over fifties, and will set them to ear his ground, and to reap his harvest, and to make his instruments of war, and instruments of his chariots. . . . And he will take your fields, and your vineyards, and your oliveyards, even the best of them, and give them to his servants."[1] In Spencer's "Descriptive Sociology," the food-getting aspect of the early history of the Hebrews is divided as follows: —

"Pre-Egyptian period: Reared sheep, oxen, asses; a slight beginning of agriculture.

Egyptian period: Love for settled abode and agriculture seems to have been implanted.

Period of the Judges: Transjordanic tribes continued shepherds; the rest passed on to agriculture.

Period of the Monarchy: Wheat and olives were cultivated in such a measure as to allow of extensive export.

Period of the Two Kingdoms: Agriculture made more extensive by terracing and watering. Wheat the chief product."

The German tribes afford another illustration of

[1] I Sam. viii. 12, 14.

the passage from the pastoral to the agricultural stage. They migrated with their cattle into Europe, and later became settled cultivators of the soil.[1]

A third illustration may be taken from the history of England. Professor W. J. Ashley [2] says on this point that "to judge from the account given by Cæsar — who had abundant opportunities of observation — the Britons, at the time of Cæsar's invasion, were still, except in Kent, in the pastoral stage. . . . When, however, we pass to the three centuries and a half of Roman rule, we can hardly help coming to the conclusion that it was during that period that England became an agricultural country."

Still another example is to be found in the history of the Greeks. "Homeric social forms," says a recent writer, "witness the long-continued presence of the nomadic stage, now passing away as a result of changed environment. It is probable that the dominant peoples of Greece and Asia Minor were a detachment of those nomadic conquerors who ever and anon swept forth from the plains of central Asia, infusing fresh blood and vigor into the societies with which they came in

[1] See Hildebrand, "Recht und Sitte auf den verschiedenen wirtschaftlichen Kulturstufen," Erster Theil, Jena, 1896; and Meitzen, "Siedelung und Agrarwesen," Berlin, 1895, Vol. I, p. 131; and compare Ashley, "Surveys Historic and Economic," New York, 1900, pp. 157–160, and pp. 115–131.

[2] In the Introduction to "The Origin of Property in Land," by Fustel de Coulanges, translated by M. Ashley, London, 1892, pp. XXIII and XXIV.

contact." [1]   It should be noted, however, that in this case the pastoral life had not resulted in domesticating those animals which are necessary to agriculture. While the Greeks were nomads they had chiefly sheep and goats, and it is probable that the ox, the horse, and the mule came to them after their western migrations and settlement.[2]

This change to a settled life with agriculture as the chief occupation is accompanied by profound

	NUMBER OF INHABITANTS PER SQUARE KILOMETER
Hunting tribes, such as the Bushmen, Patagonians, Australians	0.0017–0.0088
Hunting tribes, with some soil cultivation such as the Indians and poorer negroes . .	0.17–0.70
Fishing peoples living on the coast, as in north-western America and Polynesia . .	as many as 1.77
Pastoral nomads	0.70–1.77
Tribes with hoe culture and agriculture and some industry and commerce (inner Africa, Malays)	1.7–5.3
Purely agricultural regions of southern Europe	as many as 70
Mixed agricultural and industrial regions of central Europe.	70–106
The better cultivated regions of India, Java, China	177
Regions of the great commercial cities and industrial centres of Europe . . .	266

(Condensed from an estimate by Ratzel, quoted in Schmoller's " Grundriss der allgemeinen Volkswirtschaftslehre," p. 183.)

[1] Keller, "Homeric Society," New York, 1902, p. 30.
[2] *Ibid.*, p. 37.

changes in the whole social structure. Partly as a cause and partly as a result of the changed methods of getting a living, there is a marked increase in the density of the population, and this necessarily implies new social relations and duties. The table on page 46, showing the density of population in typical regions of the world, will emphasize the fact that the growth of civilization has meant an ever increasing closeness and complexity in the relations of man with man.

Another prominent characteristic is the great development of slavery. This had existed in previous periods, but to hunters and herdsmen, large bodies of slaves would have been a detriment, not an advantage, and therefore the slaughter of enemies was common. The Masai in East Africa, says Ratzel, are a shepherd tribe, who subsist upon herds of a fixed size, and have neither labor nor provision to spare for slaves, and hence kill their prisoners; "their neighbors, the agricultural and trading Wakamba, being able to find a use for slaves, do not kill them." [1] In the early history of Greece, slavery was a much less important institution than it became at a later period. In Homer's time, the male captives taken in war were usually slain, and only the women and children enslaved, since the social organization "was not yet strong enough to hold in subjection bodies of grown men." [2]

[1] "History of Mankind," translated by A. J. Butler, London, 1896, Vol. I, p. 123.   [2] Keller, "Homeric Society," p. 277.

But in more advanced societies, like the Egyptians, and the later Greeks and Romans, and in Europe generally during the Middle Ages, unfree labor formed a very important part of the social fabric. In China to-day slaves of both sexes are openly bought and sold all over the empire, being used chiefly in domestic work.[1] We are now convinced that, aside from any moral considerations, free labor is more efficient than slave labor; but in this early stage of industrial development, labor, it is generally maintained, had to be forced if there was to be any steady labor at all, and thus slavery may be looked upon as a necessary stage in the evolution of industrial society. It was only in later ages, when the habits of thrift and industry had been ground into the very nature of man, that the servile bonds could advantageously be removed.

The gradual growth of private landownership is a third characteristic of this period. The actual steps by which private landholding came to prevail is a matter of great dispute among the economic historians.[2] We are interested here merely in the result of the institution of a system of private property. Perhaps the magic power of the separate cultivation of the soil to increase the total product cannot be better brought out than by the following quotation, giving the experience

[1] Douglas, " Society in China," London, 1894, p. 346.

[2] For a discussion of the present status of this question see an article by G. T. Lapsley, entitled "The Origin of Property in Land," *American Historical Review*, April, 1903, Vol. VIII, p. 426.

of the early Puritans in New England. Governor Bradford, in the history "Of Plimoth Plantation," [1] after telling of the difficulty the colonists had in getting a sufficient supply of food under a system of common cultivation, says : —

"So they begane to thinke how they might raise as much corne as they could, and obtaine a beter crope then they had done, that they might not still thus languish in miserie. At length, after much debate of things, the Govr (with ye advise of ye cheefest amongest them) gave way that they should set corne every man for his owne perticuler, and in that regard trust to them selves ; in all other things to goe on in ye generall way as before. And so assigned to every family a parcell of land, according to the proportion of their number for that end, only for present use (but made no devission for inheritance) and ranged all boys & youth under some familie. This had very good success ; for it made all hands very industrious, so as much more corne was planted then other waise would have bene by any means ye Govr or any other could use, and saved him a great deall of trouble, and gave farr better contente. The women now wente willingly into ye feild, and tooke their litle-ons with them to set corne, which before would aledg weakness, and inabilitie ; whom to have compelled would have been thought great tiranie and oppression."

Experiences such as the foregoing have convinced the world of the desirability of the private cultivation of the soil. Additional reasons are perhaps needed to make conclusive the argument

[1] Reprinted in Boston, 1898, p. 162.

for private ownership with the right of inheritance, but the present writer believes that they can be found. Abuses of private landownership, such as the development of excessively large estates, are not a necessary part of the institution. We must presuppose such social regulation as will result in the holding of small estates by a relatively large part of the community. Such a class develops a spirit of independence and personality that gives stability to the whole social organism. However, there is not space at this point to enter into a discussion of this subject.

In the agricultural period there was still little development of trade. The village communities were isolated and self-sufficient. Each group raised and made the things which it needed. The wants of the people were simple, and food, clothing, and fuel could all be obtained at home. The condition of England at the time of the Norman Conquest affords a good illustration. On the manors, the needs of the community, says one writer, " were satisfied almost wholly from the ploughing and tilling of the ground and from the use and increase of the domestic animals; what handi-workers or craftsmen came into existence were mainly for the furthering of these same needs rather than for the satisfaction of new tastes or the development of new duties. . . . Probably the millard, shoemaker, smith and wright were already recognized as distinct craftsmen; but all others, such as those engaged in spinning, weaving, netting, salt-preparing, gardening, brewing, baking and cooking were, and for a considerable time continued to be, merely household servants."[1] Some trade, to be sure, existed. Salt, iron, and millstones could usually not be supplied at home,[2] and the higher classes very early secured articles of luxury from the wandering merchant. Significant of the exceptional nature of trade in the early stages of the development of industrial society is the fact that both the German word "tauschen" and the English word "barter" originally meant to "cheat."[3]

The transition stage to a freer trade between the groups is somewhat as follows: "Each proprietor still seeks, as far as possible, to gain his livelihood from the land; if his wants go beyond this, he calls into requisition any special manual skill he may possess or any particular productive advantage of his district, whether in field, forest, or water, in order to produce a surplus of some particular article. One will produce grain, another wine, a third salt, a fourth fish, a fifth linen or some other product of domestic industry."[4] Some of the more favorably situated places became the centres of the trade, and finally grew

[1] Andrews, "The Old English Manor," Baltimore, 1892, pp. 202, 237.

[2] Ashley, "An Introduction to English Economic History and Theory," Vol. I, pp. 35–36.

[3] Bücher, "Industrial Evolution," translated by S. M. Wickett, New York, 1901, p. 40.

[4] Bücher, p. 114.

into towns. Most of the eighty towns mentioned by the Domesday Survey in England "were what we should now consider but large villages : they were distinguished from the villages around only by the earthen walls that surrounded them, or the earthen mounds that kept watch over them."[1] The development of the towns as centres of trade and handicraft in Europe generally, during the Middle Ages, marks the beginning of a new stage in industrial development.

V. *The Handicraft Stage*

This stage sees the rise and decay of the gilds, and the spread of the domestic system. It is of especial interest to us because it was during this period that America was colonized. By the seventeenth century, the craft gilds had decayed in England, and it is not surprising therefore that they do not appear in America. In other respects, however, there are similarities between the early English and the early American industrial development. For example, in each case an export trade in raw products developed before the handicrafts contributed largely to the exports, Europe being to England in the thirteenth and fourteenth centuries what England was to America in the seventeenth and eighteenth. A passage from Jefferson's "Notes on Virginia" is of interest in this connection. "Our exterior commerce," he says, "has suffered very

[1] Ashley, " English Economic History," Vol. I, p. 68.

much from the beginning of the present contest. During this time we have manufactured within our families the most necessary articles of clothing. Those of cotton will bear some comparison with the same kinds of manufacture in Europe; but those of wool, flax, and hemp are very coarse and unpleasant; and such is our attachment to agriculture, and such our preference for foreign manufactures, that, be it wise or unwise, our people will certainly return as soon as they can to the raising of raw materials, and exchanging them for finer manufactures than they are able to execute themselves." [1] The following picture of an early plantation in Virginia reminds one of an old English manor that was just beginning to lose its self-sufficiency : —

"Worthy Captaine *Matthews*, an old Planter of above thirty yeers standing, one of the Counsell, and a most deserving Common-wealths-man, I may not omit to let you know this Gentlemans industry.

"He hath a fine house, and all things answerable to it ; he sowes yeerly store of Hempe and Flax, and causes it to be spun ; he keeps Weavers, and hath a *T*an-house, causes Leather to be dressed, hath eight Shoemakers employed in their trade, hath forty *Negroe* servants, brings them up to *T*rades in his house : He yeerly sowes abundance of Wheat, Barley, &c, *T*he VVheat he selleth at four shillings the bushell ; kills store of Beeves, and sells them to victuall the ships when they come thither : hath abundance of Kine, a brave Dairy, Swine great store,

[1] Edition of 1801, p. 323.

and Poltery [poultry]; he married the daughter of Sir. *Tho. Hinton*, and in a word, keeps a good house, lives bravely, and [is] a true lover of *Virginia;* he is worthy of much hononr [-our]." [1]

In the northern colonies there was a special development of fishing, lumbering, and shipbuilding. The so-called manufacturing was done chiefly in the household, and, as in England, closely allied with agriculture. Brissot de Warville, in his " New Travels in the United States of America, performed in 1788," says, "Almost all these houses are inhabited by men who are both cultivators and artisans; one is a tanner, another a shoemaker, another sells goods, but all are farmers " (p. 127). Tench Coxe, in his "View of the United States, 1787–1794" says : " Those of the tradesmen and manufacturers who live in the country, generally reside on small lots and farms from 1 acre to 20 : and not a few on farms from 20 to 150 acres; which they cultivate at leisure times, with their own hands, their wives, children, servants, apprentices, and sometimes by hired laborers. . . . This union of manufacturing and farming is found to be very convenient in the grain farms, where part of almost every day and great parts of every year can be spared from the business of the farm and employed in some mechanical handicraft or manufacturing busi-

[1] From an anonymous letter written in 1648, printed in Hart's "Source-Book of American History," p. 91. For a picture of plantation life in later times, see "The Old South," by Thomas Nelson Page, New York, 1892, pp. 143 ff.

ness " (p. 378). In Maryland, in the eighteenth century, the parson had his glebe, the lawyers and doctors had their farms. " The mechanics, fishermen, bay sailors, and petty tradesmen took a turn in the tobacco fields at planting time or helped in the wheat harvest, or in pulling and husking corn." [1]

Both countries, too, offer illustrations of another characteristic of the handicraft stage : the substitution of a money for a barter economy. The earliest of the kings in England after the Conquest received their dues from manors in kind, but Henry I found it possible to collect them in money. So, in America, the earliest taxes were paid in commodities. The following quotation from the " Records of the Colony of New Plymouth " for the year 1677 will be of interest : " The court voated that barly shalbe paied for the rate this yeer att three shillings a bushell. The proportions aboue entered [*i.e.* amount assessed to each town] are to be payed, two p̄tes of three thereof in wheat, and barly, and butter, or siluer, the wheat att 4ˢ a bushell, the barly att three shillings a bushell, and the butter att fiue pence a pound, this first payment to be made att or before the first of October next after the date heerof, and the other third p̄te to be payed in Indian corne and rye, the Indian corne att three shillings a bushell, and the rye att three shillings and six pence a bushell." [2]

The early colonial period also offers some parallel to English conditions in the minute regulation of

[1] Scharf, " History of Maryland," Vol. II, p. 58.
[2] Reprinted in Boston, 1856, Vol. V, p. 243.

economic affairs by the government. The Boston town records show that the price and size of a loaf of bread was repeatedly fixed by public authority. Competition was not relied upon to fix a price. In the records of 1635 there is a resolution: "That Mr. William Hutchinson, Mr. William Colborne and Mr. William Brenton shall sett pryces upon all cattell comodities, victuals and labourers and Workmen's Wages and that noe other prises or rates shalbe given or taken." [1] The absence of the idea of a competitive price is further shown by the following incident, related by Governor Winthrop in his Journal: A keeper of a shop in Boston was fined two hundred pounds because he took above six pence in the shilling profit. "After the court had censured him the Church of Boston called him also in question where (as before he had done in the court) he did with tears acknowledge and bewail his covetous and corrupt heart, yet making some excuse for many of the particulars which were charged against him." This gave the occasion to Mr. Cotton to lay down the rules for trading, the first of which was : " A man may not sell above the current price (*i.e.*) such a price as is usual in the time and place, and as such who knows the worth of the commodity would give for it if he had occasion to use it, as that is called current money which every man will take, etc." [2]

[1] Second Report of the Record Commissioners of Boston, p. 5.

[2] "Governor Winthrop's Journal," printed at Hartford, 1790, p. 188 ; Reprint of 1853, pp. 377–381.

These slowgoing methods of the handicraft system, where every man worked for himself with his own tools, or for other persons who were not far above him in the social scale, began to give way to the factory system in England in the last quarter of the eighteenth and in America in the first quarter of the nineteenth century. Of course, there is no intention of saying that they were entirely superseded, for many of the characteristics of one stage in industrial development are carried over into the next. In the garment trade the eighteenth century methods are being displaced with extreme slowness, and in many lines some hand-work will find a permanent place. The names we give to the various stages merely designate what is dominant in each stage.

VI. *The Industrial Stage*

The use of power manufacture, made possible by the great mechanical inventions in the latter part of the eighteenth century, brought about that far-reaching and rapid change in our industrial life which is known as the Industrial Revolution. It ushered in the era of capitalism, the wage system, and the extensive use of credit. It now became necessary for the laborers to leave their homes and assemble in factories to use the expensive machinery which each one could not own for himself. To an increasing extent, those supplying the factors of production become separated. In a particular business one set of persons might furnish the capital, an entirely different set the labor, and still a third the land. Under such conditions, the organizer, the *entrepreneur*, receives a new importance, and *captains of industry* are made possible.

There was at the same time a great change in men's ideas as to the duties of the state toward industry. Non-interference became the watchword, and the abuses that resulted in the English factories from this unregulated competition were truly appalling. In America, the evils were not so great. Chevalier, writing in 1834, testifies on this point as follows: "The cotton manufacture alone employs six thousand persons in Lowell; of this number nearly five thousand are young women from seventeen to twenty-four years of age. . . . On seeing them pass through the streets in the morning and evening and at their meal hours, neatly dressed; on finding their scarfs and shawls and green silk hoods, which they wore as a shelter from the sun and dust (for Lowell is not yet paved), hanging up in the factories amidst the flowers and shrubs, which they cultivate, I said to myself, 'This, then, is not like Manchester;' and when I was informed of the rate of their wages, I understood that it was not at all like Manchester. . . . After spending four years in the factories, they may have a little fortune of $250 or $300, when they often quit work and marry."[1] And yet the evils

[1] "Society, Manners, and Politics in the United States," Boston, ed. 1839, p. 137.

have been great here, also. At about the time when the foregoing was written, Seth Luther, a mechanic, published a pamphlet in which he sets forth the conditions in the factories as he found them.[1] The New England mills generally ran thirteen hours a day the year round, while one in Connecticut ran fifteen hours and ten minutes. At Paterson, New Jersey, the women and children had to be at work at half-past four, and sometimes were urged on by the use of the cowhide. At Mendon, Massachusetts, a boy of twelve drowned himself in a pond to escape factory labor. The United Hand Loom Weavers' Trade Association reported, in 1835, that they could earn in twelve hours but from sixty-five to seventy-one cents a day.

The reason that the evils of the change were not so great in this country was partly in the fact that there was a great supply of free land to which any who were dissatisfied with the changing conditions could turn, and partly in the fact that we had as yet not established a great economic system of any kind that could be overthrown. With us the change was an evolution rather than a revolution. The existence of a great body of unoccupied land has, indeed, been one of the most characteristic facts of our economic development. It has served as a constant force tending to keep up wages in the older regions and to furnish an outlet for the discontented element. Timothy Dwight speaks of this fact in his " Travels in New England and New

[1] See the author's " Labor Movement in America," Ch. III.

York in 1821." They had many troubles in the older regions, he says, but they would have had many more if this discontented element had remained at home. Our free land has almost disappeared, and we shall in the future have to find a new way to deal with those who are dissatisfied. That this will be no easy matter is evident when we consider that if the mainland of the United States were only half as densely populated as the German Empire is to-day, we should have over four hundred millions of people under one government.

The abuses that appeared with the factory system led, in both England and America, to a twofold reaction against the *laissez-faire* policy. Competition has been regulated by a series of factory acts and other legislation, and workmen have been stimulated to more thorough organization to secure for themselves, in the shape of higher wages, a part of the increasing wealth. But at best, a change from one stage to another must always mean loss and suffering to a part of society. The methods which were compatible with success in the slow-going handicraft stage became inappropriate in a more strenuous competitive period; and those who could not make the change lingered behind, and became what has been expressively called "the rubbish heap of the competitive system." There was once a strong feeling that those who had learned a trade had a sort of vested interest in it, and ought not to be turned out immediately when some other man could be found who might do the work more cheaply. Custom protected the incompetent to some extent from the ruthless force of competition, but later they were turned adrift to shift for themselves. In many ways, too, our habits of thought have to be changed as we pass from one stage to another. This is irksome, and we resist it for a time. The idea that a business is a man's own and ought not to be interfered with by the public is one that belongs to this early part of the industrial stage, and it has been only with extreme slowness and obstinacy that it is coming to be recognized by business men that such an attitude is an anachronism. Unquestionably the dispute between labor and capital has been aggravated by this fact. Education can do much here to make the transitions easier, because when men recognize the inevitableness of a change, they are much less apt to resist it. The necessity of discarding one's old habits of thought under new conditions can be illustrated in another way. The farmers brought up in the traditions of the individualism of New England and of the South, — where individualism is far more pronounced, — on going to the far West, where close association and coöperation were required to carry on irrigated agriculture, found that it took a long time and involved a good deal of waste to learn how to act together.

This thought has an important application at the present time. We are coming to deal more with peoples of a lower civilization, and we have to ask the question, How rapidly can they move forward to a stage of industrial civilization which is removed from them by hundreds and perhaps thousands of years? It has been necessary to modify our system of land tenure more or less in the case of the North American Indians, to assist them to make the transition from common or tribal property in land to individual property in severalty as we understand it. The question may indeed be asked if we are not expecting them to travel too rapidly. It is interesting to note that Professor J. W. Jenks, in his report upon the Philippines, does not hold that the natives are ripe for individual property in land, but recommends public ownership with leases. This illustrates very important principles of special significance to us now. For a long time in this country, under the influence of eighteenth-century philosophy, we were inclined to regard men as substantially equal, and to suppose that all could live under the same economic and political institutions. It now becomes plain that this is a theory which works disaster, and is, indeed, cruel to those who are in the lower stages, resulting in their exploitation and degradation.

Returning again to the early industrial stage, we find that, even after the idea of a regulated competition had made its way, the ideal which we attempted to follow was that the competitive struggle, even though regulated, should be maintained in every branch of production. Competition among a large number of producers, it was thought, would fix a natural price automatically. Legislators directed their efforts to maintaining competition, even in the railroad business. This general reign of competition, at first unregulated and later regulated, may be taken to characterize the first phase of the industrial era.

Within the last two or three decades a new movement has been taking place. The marked concentration of production in large establishments, commonly called the trust movement, may be regarded as a second phase of the industrial

AGRICULTURAL IMPLEMENTS [1]

YEAR	NUMBER OF ESTABLISHMENTS	AVERAGE PER ESTABLISHMENT			
		Capital	Wage Earners		Value of Product
			Average Number	Wages	
1900	715	$220,571	65	$31,400	$141,549
1890	910	159,686	43	19,898	89,310
1880	1,943	31,966	20	7,905	35,327
1870	2,076	16,780	12	5,853	25,080
1860	2,116	6,553	8	2,800	9,845
1850	1,333	2,674	5	1,626	5,133

stage. It is seen in almost every line of production, although less markedly in some than in others. It is to be observed least of all in the farming and mercantile business. To illustrate the movement, we may take the manufacture of agricultural implements. From the above table

[1] Twelfth Census Reports, "Manufactures," Pt. I, p. lxxii.

we notice an absolute decrease in the number, and a marked increase in the average size, of the establishments.

But a third phase, quite distinct from the preceding, has been attracting attention recently. It is the movement toward the integration of allied industries. For illustration, take the case of the United States Steel Corporation. Here we have united under one management the American Bridge Company, the American Sheet Steel Company, the American Steel Hoop Company, the American Steel and Wire Company, the American Tin Plate Company, the Federal Steel Company, the Lake Superior Consolidated Iron Mines, the National Steel Company, the National Tube Company, and the Carnegie Steel Company. Of the last itself, Mr. Charles M. Schwab says, in his testimony before the Industrial Commission (Vol. XIII, p. 448): " The Carnegie Company were large miners of ore — mined all the ore that they required themselves, to the extent of over 4,000,000 tons per year. They transported a large percentage of it in their own boats over the lakes; they carried a large percentage of it over their own railroad to their Pittsburg works, and manufactured it there, by the various processes, into a great variety of iron and steel articles — I think perhaps a larger general variety of steel articles than almost any other manufacturing concern."

Mr. W. F. Willoughby, in a recent article entitled "The Integration of Industry,"[1] has given the following additional illustrations: The combination of railroad and ocean transportation; the control by the Standard Oil Company of the Linseed Oil Company, which itself controls the National Lead Company; the consolidation of various lines of tobacco manufacture; the combining of production and distribution at retail by the large shoe companies; trust and security companies which perform the functions of banks, administrators of estates, real estate agents, guardians of valuables, bonding agencies, and conveyancers of property; the department store (although slightly different in principle); and finally, the English Coöperative Societies. The force at work, this writer thinks, is the same as that which impels a nation to become self-contained. This whole matter brings us to the heart of present problems, and is further discussed in Chapter V of Part I.

What the industrial age means in the way of increased facilities for the production of wealth is well shown by the elaborate investigation conducted by the United States Commissioner of Labor[2] in regard to the difference between hand labor and machine labor. For example, in 1852 the printing and folding of 480,000 pages of newspaper required 3660 hours of work at a labor cost of $447, while in 1896 the same amount of work was done in 18 hours and 30.3 minutes at a labor

[1] In the *Quarterly Journal of Economics*, Vol. XVI, p. 94.
[2] In his Thirteenth Annual Report.

cost of $6.27. Agriculture is one of the latest branches of industry to be invaded by machine methods, but the progress made in this direction is also remarkable. So early as 1851, Mr. Pusey, in his Report on Agricultural Implements in the Exhibition of 1851, estimated that in the twelve years preceding his report "a saving on outgoings or else an increase of incomings of not less than one-half" had resulted from the increased use of mechanical implements in agriculture.[1] The investigation just mentioned shows still more rapid improvement since that time. For example, to produce 40 bushels of corn in 1855 required 38 hours and 45 minutes of work at a labor cost of $3.63; while in 1894 that amount could be produced by 15 hours and 7.8 minutes of work at a labor cost of only $1.51. Whether human well-being has on the whole increased in the same proportions may be doubted, but after taking into account all of the evils the new industrial system has brought, there is without doubt a large balance in its favor, with unbounded possibilities for the future.

So far we have been viewing the development of society from the standpoint of production. Other viewpoints are of course possible. One writer[2] has taken as his principle of classification the length of time which elapses between the production and the consumption of the goods, and

[1] Quoted in Hearn's "Plutology," London, 1864, p. 172.
[2] Bücher, "Industrial Evolution," p. 89.

from this standpoint he gets the following three stages : —

1. The stage of independent economy.
2. The stage of town economy.
3. The stage of national economy.

The stage of domestic independent production is that in which the household is an independent group, a well-nigh self-sufficient economic group. Goods are produced in and by the household group, and are consumed by this group. Economic self-sufficiency is the ideal. This stage existed in classical Greece, and is found in all earlier industrial civilizations. The stage of town economy is that in which handicrafts are developed. Goods are produced by artisans for customers, so that the producer meets the consumer without intermediaries. The village shoemaker taking orders from individual customers and making their shoes for them is a type of this stage. Exchange takes place and commerce exists, but on a comparatively simple scale. The economic relations among men are relatively few and simple. In the stage of national economy, production is conducted on a large scale, and the goods pass through several hands before they reach the consumer. We are now in this stage; and, one may add, the next stage, according to this view, would be world economy. The business world is becoming more and more cosmopolitan. The industrial ties binding nations together are becoming closer. The money market is truly a world market. We hear of the invasion of foreign countries by the captains of industry, and of the formation of world trusts.

If we look at the evolution of industrial society with respect to the tranfers of goods, we may discover three distinct periods, and these follow each other chronologically. This was first worked out in detail by the German economist, Bruno Hildebrand.[1] We have, first, an early stage preceding the use of money, which may be designated as barter or truck economy. Then we have the stage in which money becomes prominent, and to this we may give the term money economy, and following money economy, we have a third period called credit economy. Barter exists in the period designated as money economy, but what characterizes this period is the use of money, which increasingly replaces barter. Similarly, in our own time, the third period, money is still used, but credit dominates the period to such an extent that money has been well called the small change of commerce.

When we look at the evolution of society from the standpoint of labor, we find first of all the labor of women and the slaughter of enemies. The slaughter of enemies was in more advanced civilizations quite generally replaced by slavery. Then we observe a transition to a modified form of slavery, or serfdom, in Europe generally during the Middle Ages. When the laborer secures his

[1] " Jahrbücher für Nationalökonomie," 1864, Vol. II, p. 1.

freedom, he is regulated by custom and status in making his individual contracts. This was the condition in the handicraft period. Later, as the force of custom wanes, there is at first little interference in the making of his contracts, and then regulation to an increasing extent by statute, and finally, we have collective bargaining regulated still more by statute. This transition from the individual contract to group contract which is now taking place is, like all transitional stages, accompanied with disturbance and pain. Processes of readjustment in human relationships always have brought suffering, and doubtless always will bring suffering, although the suffering may be greatly mitigated by a better will and a higher intelligence.

Recently Professor F. H. Giddings[1] has proposed a new classification. He rejects the common classification, not that it is untrue, but that it is destitute of any real meaning.[2] He divides all economies into three classes, the Organic, the Instinctive, and the Rational. We may pass over the first two, as practically all human activity falls within the last. The Rational Economy is again divided into (1) Ceremonial and (2) Business Economies. Within the first there are three phases,

[1] In an article entitled "The Economic Ages," *Political Science Quarterly*, Vol. XVI, p. 193.

[2] The present writer differs emphatically as to the utility of the older classification. It furnishes a convenient framework within which to arrange our knowledge, and elucidates the progress of industrial society.

— the Luck, the Magic, and the Sacrificial Economies, — in which there is a progressive mental development from reliance on mere conjecture, through reasoning by analogy, to logical reasoning in which there is no careful examination of the premises. The mark of the business economy is inductive reasoning, and here again are three phases, a Slave, a Trade, and a Capitalistic Economy. This way of looking at the matter brings out the psychological element, and one is certainly compelled to admit that industrial evolution means something more than a mere improvement in technical processes. It means at the same time changing human beings, mentally and morally.

These various classifications are not only not antagonistic, but they are all necessary to a complete view of industrial evolution. This will be made clear by the table on the following page.

In conclusion, it must be repeated that a table of this kind is helpful if used with discretion ; that otherwise it is misleading. The transitions from one stage to another are slow, and old forms persist when a new period in industrial evolution has made its appearance. The differences between the stages are best understood by comparing each one when it is fully developed. Between the fully developed periods of each stage there is a transitional growth. The table also gives that which is dominant and characteristic in each stage. It has already been stated, for example, that money is used in the stage of credit economy, but that it

THE ECONOMIC STAGES

From the Standpoint of Production	From Bücher's Standpoint	From Hildebrand's Standpoint	From the Labor Standpoint		From Giddings's Standpoint [1]
1. Hunting and Fishing	Independent Domestic Economy	Truck Economy	Slaughter of Enemies, Woman's Labor, and Beginning of Slavery	Ceremonial	Luck / Magic
2. Pastoral					Sacrificial
3. Agricultural			Slavery and Serfdom		Slave Labor
4. Handicraft	Town Economy	Money Economy	Free Labor governed by Custom	Business Economy	Trade
5. Industrial (1) Universal Competition as an ideal (2) Concentration (3) Integration	National Economy (World Economy) [2]	Credit Economy	Individual Contract with Increasing Regulation by Statute / Group Contract and Regulation by Statute		Capitalistic

[1] Probably Professor Giddings would not himself be willing to state at just what points in industrial evolution these divisions come, and manifestly there is a considerable overlapping. All that the present author intends to say is that there is a general correspondence in the stages as indicated in the table.

[2] Added by the present author.

is credit which especially characterizes the later stage. The significance of this fact is brought out by recent discussions on money. Many persons who have engaged in the popular discussion of this topic seem to have overlooked the fact that we have reached a period of credit economy, and that what is essential above everything else is that credit should rest upon a sound foundation, and that, inasmuch as money is but the " small change of business," an increase or decrease in the supply of money is a small matter as compared with the volume of credit. A sound basis of credit must, above everything else, be provided, and the money question is to be viewed very largely from the viewpoint of its influence upon credit. This is mentioned to illustrate the significance of the stages.

A word or two further may be said about the stages when viewed from the labor standpoint. Manual labor goes back to slavery, and throughout the world we find development from slavery through various half-free forms to a condition of freedom. Slavery was an outcome very largely of war ; conquered enemies in the early ages were enslaved. Preceding slavery we have, as has been pointed out, slaughter of enemies. Manual toil also was in early ages performed largely by woman ; consequently, the slaughter of enemies and woman's labor are characteristic features of the early stage in the development of labor. Man toiled also in the manner which has been indicated in the present chapter. There are also, in primitive society, variations in the toil performed by men, but it has not been compatible with the purposes of this book to enter into these variations fully. The endeavor is made in this Part I to give a broad general survey only of the evolution of industrial society.

CHAPTER IV

ECONOMIC CLASSES

WE have seen in previous chapters that the
evolution of society has meant an ever increasing
differentiation. From another standpoint, this
means that there is a greater and greater variety
in the groups of persons having common characteristics. Race, nationality, ability, education,
moral qualities, religious beliefs, manners, wealth,
and occupation, each affords a basis for a different
classification. But, ordinarily, when we speak of
classes in society, we have in mind those class
divisions which affect the social intercourse of
people, and which give them a higher or lower
rank. The "Century Dictionary" defines a class
as "An order or rank of persons; a number of
persons having certain characteristics in common,
as equality in rank, intellectual influence, education, property, occupation, habits of life, etc." In
the present discussion we are concerned with the
influence exerted by the economic organization
and constitution of society [1] on the formation of
class distinctions. It is to these that we refer
when we speak of economic classes.

[1] The distribution of wealth is included.

74

ECONOMIC CLASSES

In the earliest stages of society, we have seen, the women are the principal workers. Later, slaves are forced to labor for the community. Then we find the workers becoming free, but at first they stand at the bottom of the social scale. Among the Greeks and Romans, commerce and industry were considered unworthy pursuits for a citizen. In the caste system of India the industrial class occupies a position only one grade higher than that of the servile class. Step by step the wealth-producing members of society have won for themselves social recognition, and to-day we in America look with growing disfavor upon a man who lives upon an inherited income without engaging in some " useful " occupation. But the workers have themselves become differentiated, and increasingly so with the growing complexity of modern business life.

It has often been said that we have no classes in America. Our federal Constitution says that no title of nobility shall be granted either by the United States or by any state. The law is supposed to guarantee every man an equal vote, regardless of his property, his education, his birth, or even his color. Every child, we have been fond of saying, has an equal chance of rising to the highest position either in the political or the industrial world. " In the United States," said De Tocqueville, writing in 1833, " professions are more or less laborious, more or less profitable ; but they are never either high or low : every honest calling is honorable." To be sure, even in his day there were rich and poor, but, he remarks, " the class of rich men does not exist; for these rich individuals have no feeling or purposes in common, no mutual traditions or mutual hopes; there are individuals, therefore, but no definite class." [1]

This same writer, however, also gave a warning. The extensive subdivision of labor and the resulting large-scale production, he saw, was working a change. In this connection he observes: " The master and workman have then here no similarity, and their differences increase every day. They are only connected as two rings at the extremities of a long chain. Each of them fills the station which is made for him and which he does not leave: the one is continually, closely, and necessarily dependent upon the other, and seems as much born to obey as that other is to command. What is this but Aristocracy ? " [2]

Some fifty years later another foreign observer wrote : " There are no struggles between privileged and unprivileged orders, not even that perpetual strife of rich and poor which is the oldest disease of civilized states. One must not pronounce broadly that there are no classes, for in parts of the country social distinctions have begun to grow up. But for political purposes classes scarcely exist. No one of the questions which now agitate the nation is a question between rich and poor.

[1] De Tocqueville, " Democracy in America," Boston, 1873, Vol. II, pp. 186 and 196.   [2] *Ibid.*, p. 195.

Instead of suspicion, jealousy, and arrogance embittering the relations of classes, good feeling and kindliness reign." [1] This was written in 1888, but the author, in a later edition of his book (1894) suggests that possibly the view might seem too roseate, although he hesitates to " let matured conclusions be suddenly modified by passing events."

In recent years we have been hearing much about the struggle between the laboring class and the capitalist class. There are those who think that the words which Karl Marx and Friedrich Engels wrote, in the " Communist Manifesto," in 1848, find support in the present economic conditions in the United States. These writers said : " The history of all hitherto existing society is the history of class struggles. Freeman and slave, patrician and plebeian, lord and serf, guild-master and journeyman, in a word, oppressor and oppressed, stood in constant opposition to one another, carried on an uninterrupted, now hidden, now open, fight, that each time ended, either in revolutionary reconstitution of society at large or in the common ruin of the contending classes. In the earlier epochs of history we find almost everywhere a complicated arrangement of society in various orders, a manifold gradation of social rank. In ancient Rome we have patricians, knights, plebeians, slaves; in the Middle Ages feudal lords, vassals, guild-masters, journeymen, apprentices,

[1] Bryce, "The American Commonwealth," 3d ed., Vol. II, p. 599.

serfs; in almost all ·of these classes, again, subordinate gradations. The modern bourgeois society that has sprouted from the ruins of feudal society has not done away with class antagonisms. . . . Society as a whole is more and more splitting up into two great hostile camps, into two great classes, directly facing each other, Bourgeoisie and Proletariat."

Within the past year it has been possible for a writer to attract widespread attention by his comparison of our present industrial organization with the feudal organization of the Middle Ages.[1] Such views are greatly exaggerated, but they serve to remind us of the ancient philosopher's warning that momentous changes may be taking place within a society long before there is any apparent change in the outward forms of government. The characteristics which we have been associating with the idea of democratic America may after all belong merely to the early days of this country. Indeed, class divisions have to-day a greater significance in the older parts of the country than they do in the newer. The farther west one goes, the more democratic becomes society. The author has found there are social differences even in the middle West which would be scorned in most places in Colorado. Let us inquire, then, what modern industry is doing in the way of erecting social barriers.

One great cleavage that we see in this country

[1] W. J. Ghent: "Our Benevolent Feudalism."

is the separation of the farming classes from the industrial workers proper. We have already seen that the early "manufacturers" were at the same time farmers, but gradually city life has become differentiated from country life. This separation has not, however, been of any great significance in the formation of social classes. To be sure, those living in the city have looked upon themselves as a little more cultured than their country cousins, but the latter have no feeling of inferiority. We certainly cannot speak here of higher and lower classes. Such differences between city and country as exist may, moreover, be expected to become somewhat less in the future. The growing use of the telephone, the extensive building of interurban electric roads, and the improvement in the country schools are making the distinction less sharp.

Another broad division is often made by separating the employers from the employed. This classification has been growing in importance. In Washington's administration, let us say, it at least would not have been unreasonable for an ordinary laboring man to expect to become the manager of a business of his own. Nowadays it is absurd to hold out to the masses of men such a prospect. The few may rise, as the few may draw prizes in a lottery, but it is foolish for an ordinary workman to look forward to great wealth or to the ownership of an independent business. There are, for example, over a million persons engaged in the railway business in the United States, but less than one per cent of them are officers of any sort, let alone being president of the railway.

Professor Thorstein Veblen, of the University of Chicago, has drawn a careful distinction between what he calls the industrial and pecuniary classes.[1] The former class comprises the actual workers in the factories, who come in contact chiefly with the technical processes of industry, while the latter class contains those individuals who are engaged in buying and selling, making contracts, etc. The pecuniary management, he says, has been passing into the hands of a relatively decreasing class, whose contact with the industrial classes grows continually less immediate. This difference of employment is leading to differences in habits of thought, and this growing unfamiliarity of the working classes with the pecuniary side of business may account in some measure, Professor Veblen thinks, for their improvidence, their disrespect for private property, and the growth of socialism. The distinction is interesting, but its significance may be exaggerated.

Again, we may divide the workers according to their kind of occupation. We have the bakers, the barbers, the blacksmiths, the carpenters, the coopers, the glass bottle blowers, the machinists, etc., etc. The members of such groups as these will form associations, develop class sympa-

[1] In an article entitled " Industrial and Pecuniary Employments," Publication of the American Economic Association, 1901, p. 190.

thies, and work together for their common interests, but it cannot be said that these are harmful
or undesirable class distinctions. They would
necessarily exist in any society in which each man
engaged in that occupation for which he possessed
the greater aptitude.

So, also, with the stratifications which appear
within any business itself. The existence of su-
perintendents, managers, and foremen is indispen-
sable in a large business. Extensive coöperation
necessarily means gradations in authority, but
these in themselves are not an evil, for if we could
be sure that the higher positions are filled by
those who are best fitted for them, we should have
merely the recognition of a natural aristocracy of
merit, which philosophers have always approved.

One of the chief questions concerning economic
classes is whether present economic conditions are
such as actually result in the selection of the best
for the highest positions. Is there a real equality
of opportunity for all of the members of society to
show what they can do? Vast differences in
wealth stand in the way of such equality, for,
though a rich man's son may be at a disadvan-
tage so far as temptation to idleness is concerned,
there is simply no comparison between his opportunities and those of a poor man's son. Differences in wealth are, indeed, the most potent
cause in the formation of social classes, not merely
because great wealth is a mark of distinction, but
because of the opportunities it brings of develop-

ing one's powers, and also because, as great wealth persists, habits of life and thought are formed which necessarily separate class from class. In many a city in the United States there is no individual or family with an income of $40,000 a year, but there are circles in the United States in which a person can move with difficulty with an income of that amount. Perhaps it should not be so; but, as a matter of fact, when differences in wealth pass a certain point — vague and shifting, to be sure, but real — they do operate as a social barrier, and prevent the growth of fraternal feeling. This has been recognized by philosophers from time immemorial.

This brings us to a feature of present economic conditions which is doing much to raise up social barriers, namely, monopoly power in private hands. Looking at the matter in whichever way we please, the monopolist is a privileged person, and monopolists constitute a privileged class, as truly as the nobility of old England or Germany; indeed, the position of the ancient nobility is, comparatively speaking, a small matter.[1] Monopoly power is a social force which separates men out from one another into well-defined classes, and thus lays a basis for dangerous agitation. First, it gives us a privileged class of men, receiving higher profits than those with which

---

[1] The successful monopolist can sometimes buy a title; frequently he can give his daughter a dowry which, with other opportunities, will enable her to marry a man with a high and historically distinguished title.

the unprivileged must be content. In the second place, the monopolist promotes the formation of classes among consumers, as a result of the action of monopoly price. Monopoly price means class price, whereas competitive price is uniform, and, if we may use such an expression, democratic in its action. Where we have perfect competition working, we have one uniform price charged for the same article at the same time. But monopoly price, free from the restraints of competition, is the price which will yield the largest returns. The restraint upon an increase of price comes only through a diminution of sales. We cannot go into this matter at length here, but a little reflection will show that this fact must mean class price. The price which is most profitable for one class is not the price which is most profitable for another class in a community. Consequently the monopolist attempts to find some method of dividing the community into classes, and asking of each class that price which is most profitable. This will result in a charge of a high price for those who are comparatively weak and feeble, and unable to resist imposition. In some cases, also, it will operate to establish a high price for the wealthy, and a comparatively low price for poorer people. There is no manifest unwillingness on the part of men to fleece the wealthy whenever they get a chance. The poor, even, evince this inclination, for it must by no means be supposed that in society we have to do simply with good poor men, and bad rich men — far from it. The formation of class price increases among us with the growth of monopoly. One of the best illustrations is offered by the large number of kinds of tickets which our railways are offering, in order thereby to find that price which is most profitable for each class in the community. For cities within fifty miles of Chicago, along the line of one of our great railway systems, the author has counted six different kinds of tickets, each ticket representing a class price.

There is still another way in which monopoly leads to the formation of classes, and that is through the varying treatment which monopolists accord to their customers, otherwise than in the matter of price. The general rule is that the strong are the favored, as may be seen in the discriminations made by the railways in favor of large shippers.

In conclusion, it must be said that classes in modern times have chiefly an economic and not a political basis, and that if we take any definition which we will as a guide, we must acknowledge that we have classes in the United States. We have groups of individuals who possess common characteristics. They have their own peculiar habits of body and of mind, and their own peculiar needs. The farmer has his way of looking at things, the merchant another way. The wage-earner, especially as he develops, as he is doing, class consciousness, has still other ways of doing things and viewing affairs. The chief classification in our own day is that which is caused, on the one hand, by variations in wealth, and on the other, by a separation between the employed and the employers. All this comes about naturally, as the result of the evolution of industrial society. We have different psychical worlds, and this is brought out very clearly whenever a great strike takes place. Those who read with approval the great daily newspapers of our time have their world of ideas and interests, and this is a different world of ideas and interests from that to which those belong who read with approval the so-called labor press. If one passes from one class of newspapers to the other one finds an entire change of viewpoint, and what appears black to the one is white to the other. Those whose feelings, sympathies, and interests are the feelings, sympathies, and interests of the employing class, in reading a great New York daily, will nod their heads approvingly and say, "Yes, that is true." On the other hand, those who entertain the views of the working classes, and sympathize with them in their struggles, will read with approval the diametrically opposite utterances of the labor press. How could there be a more clearly cut social cleavage?

The effects of classes are both good and evil. They are good because they tend to develop different gifts and capacities, and to produce a rich and diversified civilization. They are evil because their natural tendency is, as they become sharply differentiated, to separate man from his fellows; and this is a bad thing. But as we shall see more clearly as we proceed in the present book, there are forces at work which tend to bring men of different classes together. The movement is by no means all in one direction. The ideal is that of a friendly and harmonious coöperation of classes, with the free passage from one class to another, in accordance with gifts, and the union of all classes in one social body. There are forces at work among us, and powerful forces, for the accomplishment of this ideal. It rests with us to see whether or not the forces of social union shall triumph over the forces of social disintegration.

CHAPTER V

As we look back over the course of economic evolution, we observe certain general lines of development standing out with especial prominence. One of these is the growth and modification of the idea of property. In the earliest of the economic stages, we have seen, the idea is wanting, not merely of private, but also of public property. The idea of ownership does not exist. In the pastoral stage, ownership in movable goods is recognized, and in the agricultural stage, landownership makes its appearance. To-day the idea of property is so thoroughly ingrained in our habits of thought that it must be regarded as one of the fundamental facts in our economic life. But it has reached no final form. It is continually being modified; and we may note here some of the present tendencies along this line. In the first place, there is an increasing mass of free goods, especially free intellectual goods. Every year sees an addition to the number of great ideas that may be utilized by any one who cares to appropriate them. To be sure, we grant patents and copyrights, but they are but temporary. In a very true sense there exists a body of knowledge that is a social heritage handed down from one generation to another, constantly increasing, and free to all. A second tendency is the restriction of the extent of private property, and, generally speaking, an extension of public property. The world over we notice an increase in public property in forest lands. The increase in play-grounds for children, in public parks, in public libraries, and in the municipal ownership of "public utilities," affords other illustrations. In the third place, there is a clear development in the social side of private property. More and more the idea that private property is a social trust has made its way, and it is now recognized that the arguments in favor of private property are based chiefly upon the benefits which society derives therefrom. Again, new forms of property are continually appearing. Patents and copyrights are comparatively recent in the world's history. Good will in business is often bought and sold. Certain new rights very much akin to private property are also being recognized, such as the right to be protected against injury, which seems to be implied in the employer's liability acts. We are hearing more, also, of the right to work. Finally, we notice changes in the mode of acquisition of private property. In earlier times, force played a larger part in the acquisition of property, but we are coming to insist more and more that it shall be won by service. There is a general movement to restrict the sources of unearned incomes, such as monopoly profits, and the increasing taxation of inheritances has some significance in this connection.

The evolution of forethought is another one of these general lines of development that stand out conspicuously. We have seen how little of it was to be found among the American Indians, and probably we can say that the advance of civilization involves a continuous and uninterrupted development in the habit of taking thought for the future. The increasing importance which individuals attach to the future is at least a partial explanation of the fall in the rate of interest. But socially, we Americans, on account of the newness of our economic life, show a lack of forethought with reference to the use of our resources when we are contrasted with older civilizations. A German commissioner at the World's Fair in Chicago, when asked for his most marked impression of the United States, after some hesitation, on being pressed, said this, " You are a nation of robbers." He went on to speak about the way in which we are squandering our resources and robbing future generations. We have a certain amount of individual forethought, but we have less social forethought.

But perhaps the one fact in the evolution of society that becomes clearer and clearer as time passes, is that coöperation is the great law of social life growth. Men learn to act together in increasingly large numbers for increasingly numerous purposes. Individualism in production, exchange, distribution, and even consumption, gradually yields to coöper-ation.[1] Early man produces for himself, and in his own group consumes that which has been pro-duced and worked up in the household. He goes his way with economically little regard to the ac-tivities of other households. Every step forward in his progress means an increasing number of relations with other households, until we come to a time when very little which the ordinary indi-vidual consumes is produced by him, but reaches him as a result of the activities of thousands and hundreds of thousands, and even millions of men, who are working for him, while he serves them. The whole world becomes a vast network, in which each serves all and all serve each.

Another great social law which becomes appar-ent in the course of evolution is this : *we pass over from unconscious social coöperation to conscious social coöperation.* At first, men act together be-cause each one is pursuing his own ends, and they are scarcely aware that they are coöperating with each other. But this changes with a growth in the complexity and magnitude of the industrial units of society. Conscious coöperation in indus-try is only one part of the developing self-con-sciousness of society. Society sets before itself

[1] Among the Iroquois each individual ate by himself, sitting or standing, and where most convenient to the person. They also separated as to the time of eating, the men coming first, and then the women and children by themselves. Morgan, " Houses and House Life of the American Aborigines," contributions to *North American Ethnology*, Vol. IV, p. 99.

purposes, and attempts to achieve them through social action. As our life becomes social, this method
for the achievement of our purposes, namely, social
action, is inevitable. We have in this an explanation of many modern phenomena which seem
strange to those who do not have the right clew
for their explanation. At first, social efforts for
the attainment of social purposes are necessarily
crude, and failures are more common than suc-
cesses. Society, like a child, must learn to walk
without stumbling. We have our Granger movements in our attempts to regulate those agencies
of social coöperation which we call the railways.
A failure of early movements does not, and cannot, lead to an abandonment of social efforts. The
Granger legislation makes way for state railway
commissions and the Interstate Commerce Commission. This represents a higher form of social
effort, but by no means a final form. These various commissions must receive a much higher development, or make way for something else, possibly
even public ownership, but this remains to be
seen.

That which is especially characteristic of the
most modern phase of social evolution is the effort
to secure harmony and unity of action among great
industrial establishments, in order to achieve thereby
the largest results with the least output of energy.
The avoidance of waste of economic energy is, in
other words, the great underlying principle of the
present phase of industrial evolution. In the earlier

phase of the industrial stage a marvellous order was achieved in a single industrial establishment; but each establishment went its own way with little regard to other industrial establishments. The result was disharmony and loss. The critics of society found many points of attack in this contradiction between the harmonious coöperation of all the parts of a single establishment, and the lack of organized and harmonious working among the various establishments. It was this particular aspect of production which led the socialists to speak of the planlessness of private capitalistic production. Planlessness is, indeed, one of the great words in the socialist critique, but one heard somewhat less frequently since the trust era began. Each one, they said, is dependent upon all others who are producing for the same market the things which he is producing. All manufacturers of shoes are dependent upon all other manufacturers of shoes, inasmuch as all these others are competitors. But no one, it was argued, knows what his competitors are doing, and each one is therefore working in the dark. The result of this unorganized production of competitors must therefore be overproduction, stagnation, and industrial ruin brought about by the economic crisis. This is but a rough sketch of the criticism, and takes up but a single line. Nowadays, the socialists insist more upon bad distribution as the cause of crises. Unquestionably, this lack of harmony was a weakness which intelligent men, desiring progress, must endeavor to correct. To secure harmonious action among producers and to avoid needless waste, two methods have been followed: the first, the method of public action; the second, the method of private action.

Railways in Germany and in the United States offer an excellent illustration. The waste and disadvantages of planlessness in the railway world early became obvious, and in Germany the states have undertaken to secure unity, and that chiefly through public ownership and operation. The various German states have not all moved with equal rapidity in this matter. Prussia long tried the experiment of a mixed system of public and private ownership before, about twenty years ago, abandoning that for an almost exclusive system of publicly owned and operated railways. The state of Würtemberg, however, from the beginning had a unified and exclusive system of public railways, placed under the control of a railway manager of exceptional ability. In the United States, clearsighted and long-headed men, powerful personalities like Commodore Vanderbilt, saw, with equal clearness, the advantages of unity; and, through his own private effort, seconded by able lieutenants, Vanderbilt began a movement for consolidation and unification which yielded him one of the largest fortunes up to that time known in the history of the world. What has taken place in railways has taken place in the case of those other undertakings which we class together roughly as either natural monopolies or public utilities. This method of public ownership we may perhaps designate as the Teutonic method; and the method of private ownership with attempted public control over private corporations owning and operating undertakings of the class in question, we may designate as the French method or, more properly speaking, the Latin method. It is the method which characterized this country in the nineteenth century, and we might perhaps with equal propriety call it the nineteenth-century American method. Whether or not it will be the twentieth-century method is open to doubt. We are Teutonic rather than French or Latin in our modes of thought and action. In the case of local public utilities, at any rate, we are rapidly extending the system of public ownership in order that we may secure the benefits of unified and systematic production, although the restriction of monopoly profits has been the chief consideration in this last case.

The efforts to secure unity and harmony in the relations of manufacturing establishments to one another have, however, been almost altogether private in this country as well as in other countries. The United States leads the world in the trust movement, and the most gigantic, perhaps one should say colossal, achievement along this line is found in the United States Steel Corporation. The industrial question which overshadows in importance all other questions is this : Is indus-

trial evolution naturally leading to the domination
of substantially all the great fields of industry by
monopoly? In an earlier chapter attention was
called to the theory of industrial evolution advanced
by Karl Marx. More than fifty years ago he uttered
words which to many, even non-socialists, now seem
like a prophecy. Marx predicted that the business
units in production would continually increase in
magnitude, until in each branch of industry
monopoly would emerge from the struggle of
interests. When this happened he thought that
private monopoly would be replaced by public
monopoly; in other words, that pure social ownership and operation of all great industries would be
substituted for private ownership and operation,
and thus would dawn the era of socialism. Here
are the impressive words in which a generation
ago he expressed this thought: —

"With the continually decreasing number of the
magnates of capitalism, who usurp and monopolize
all the advantages of the changed form of production, there is an accompanying increase in the mass
of misery, of oppression, of bondage, of degradation, of exploitation; but there also arises a revolt
of an increasing class of laborers, who have been
schooled, united, and disciplined by the mechanism
of the capitalistic processes of production. The
monopoly of capital becomes a shackle to the
method of production, under and with which it
has grown up. The concentration of the means
of production and the association of laborers

95

reach a point where they are incompatible with their capitalistic shell. The shell is broken. The death knell of capitalistic private property sounds. The expropriateurs are expropriated." [1] The advocates of the trust frequently use arguments precisely like these of the socialists in pointing out the benefits of trust production, and maintain that the advantages of system and unity are so vast that in the end the trust method will dominate every great industrial field.

A discussion of the various aspects of this question brings before us, as subordinate questions, nearly all the pressing economic problems of our day. It is hard to see how we can have any clear opinions in regard to public policy, until we have satisfied ourselves in regard to the question whether or not there are natural laws in the industrial world governing industrial evolution, and bringing about inevitably a reign of monopoly, either private or public.

In considering this question, we must first of all sharply distinguish between large-scale production and monopolistic production. This is something which the author has been iterating, and reiterating, for the past fifteen years, or more. Many others have also been saying the same thing, and it seems now to be generally understood. It is, indeed, strange that it should ever have been difficult to understand the difference between vast pro-

[1] "Das Kapital," 2te Aufl., S. 793. Quoted in Ely's "French and German Socialism," pp. 177-178.

duction and monopolistic production. One of our great retail stores, like Marshall Field's, or Mandel Brothers', in Chicago, or Wanamaker's, in Philadelphia or New York City, represents very large scale production, but along with this large scale production there is the sharpest kind of competition.

Competition is the foundation of our present social order. Our legal system rests upon competition as a basis. The great legal decisions in England and America assume, either implicitly or explicitly, that competition is a pillar of the social order. Competition, along with large scale production, brings its own problems, but they are easy of solution as compared with the problems of monopoly, because competition is compatible with private property in capital, and with private production. Where competition exists, the problem is its regulation in such a manner as to secure its benefits, and to remove, where it is possible, and where it is not possible, to mitigate, its evils. What is needed for competition, especially, is to raise its moral and ethical level.

But we find among us widespread monopoly as a result of industrial evolution, and this has brought evils of another sort, which will be discussed in a later chapter.[1]

There seems to be something inevitable in all these general tendencies that we have been sketching. When we have said all that we can about the

[1] See *infra*, Pt. II, Ch. IV.

power of the individual will, we still find that there are great social forces which compel us to act along certain lines. The steady growth of population brings with it new problems, more complex social relations, and we are forced to adjust ourselves accordingly. The momentous changes resulting from the industrial revolution have come about without the anticipation or express will of society; we could not turn back now to former conditions if we would; all that we can do is to attempt to control and take advantage of these new forces. The most general statement of our industrial problem is this: How shall we retain the advantages of associated effort with freedom of movement and a socially desirable distribution of products? This is a task which demands all our best powers and our best purposes, with a willingness to sacrifice private ease and comfort for the public good.

Reference has been made to the growing co-operation among men. This means at the same time increasing dependence of man upon man, but this increasing dependence is not burdensome, provided it is mutual. If it is one-sided dependence, it may become virtually slavery under the name of freedom. Dependence must mean interdependence. The multiplying relations of men with one another give us a new economic world. These relations require regulation, in order to preserve freedom. The regulation by the power of the state of these industrial and other social relations existing among men is an essential condition of freedom. Herbert Spencer, looking at the political regulation of economic relations, speaks of a coming slavery,[1] but he overlooks the fact that with the increasing dependence of man upon man in modern society, this dependence becomes one-sided, and results in slavery if these relations are not regulated. This is the explanation of the fact that every civilized nation in the world finds it necessary to regulate to an increasing extent the industrial relations existing among men. Free contract alone, that is to say, unregulated, can only result in a degrading dependence of some men upon others, and consequently social degradation. On the other hand, through regulated association come freedom and individuality.

[1] Spencer's article, "The Coming Slavery," and three other articles similar in character have been reprinted under the title, "The Man *versus* The State." This forms an appendix to the abridged and revised edition of "Social Statics," New York, 1897.

CHAPTER VI

In the foregoing chapters we have been discussing economic development in general terms. It will be of help to consider also some statistical evidence of the industrial progress in the United States.

We have seen how industrial evolution has meant a steady increase in population. Herein American experience but repeats the world's experience.

From 1790 to 1900 our numbers have increased over nineteen fold, although in the last half-century the rate of increase has been declining. The density of population, that is, the number of inhabitants per square mile, has also steadily increased, except in the two decades 1800–1810 and 1840–1850, when large additions were made to our territory. But the figures for the density in each geographical division are more instructive. They show very clearly the gradual westward movement of the population. The following table shows the remarkable growth in population with respect to numbers and density : [1]—

---

[1] Twelfth Census, " Population," Pt. I, pp. xx, xxxiii, and lxxxiii.

| | United States and Territories | | | Density of Population in each Geographical Division | | | | |
Census Years	Total Population (Excluding Hawaii, Alaska, Indian Territory, Indian Reservations, etc.)	Per cent the urban [1] is of total	Density	North Atlantic	South Atlantic	North Central	South Central	Western
1790	3,929,214	3.4	4.9	12.1	8.6		0.6	
1800	5,308,483	4.0	6.6	16.3	10.7	0.2	1.9	
1810	7,239,881	4.9	3.7	21.5	12.5	0.4	2.3	
1820	9,638,453	4.9	4.8	26.9	14.3	1.1	4.0	
1830	12,866,020	6.7	6.4	34.2	13.6	2.1	5.9	
1840	17,069,453	8.5	8.4	41.7	14.6	4.4	8.7	
1850	23,191,876	12.5	7.9	53.2	17.4	7.2	7.1	0.2
1860	31,443,321	16.1	10.8	65.4	20.0	12.1	10.7	0.5
1870	39,818,449 [2]	20.9	13.3	75.9	21.8	17.2	11.9	0.8
1880	50,155,783	22.6	17.3	89.5	28.3	23.0	16.5	1.5
1890	62,622,250	29.2	21.2	107.4	33.0	29.7	18.3	2.6
1900	75,568,686	33.1	25.6	129.8	38.9	34.9	23.1	3.5

The North Central states have about the same density now that the North Atlantic had in 1830, and the latter had a greater density in 1790 than the Western states have now. The movement of the population from the country to the city is shown in the column giving the percentage of urban to total population. At the present time 33.1 per cent of the people of the United States live in cities of 8000 inhabitants or more.

But an increase in population is not in itself a desirable thing unless it also means an increase in the well-being of the individuals. Were the

---

[1] In cities of 8000 or more.   [2] Corrected population.

seventy-five millions of 1900 better off than the five millions of 1800? So far as material resources are concerned there can be no question about an affirmative answer. Notwithstanding the fact that the population has increased in geometrical ratio, having, roughly speaking, doubled every twenty-five years, our command over material goods has increased at a still greater rate. We do not have trustworthy statistics in regard to the total increase in wealth, measured in terms of money value; and if we did, this would not be an accurate index of the growth in well-being, for, leaving out of account questions of distribution and the changing value of money, we must remember that a large increase in the supply of goods may mean a decrease in total value through a lowering of price, but it must mean an increase in total utility. For example, the cotton crop in 1898 of 11,189,000 bales had a smaller value than the 9,143,000 bales of the next year. The increasing money value of land in cities means a growth of population, but does it always indicate a corresponding increase in well-being? If the canals of the United States should be transformed into natural waterways, our well-being would be the same or greater, but the money estimate of wealth would be less. But taking the statistics as we find them, they do show an increase in per capita wealth. While too unreliable to serve as a basis for accurate comparisons, they may be quoted as a partial confirmation of our general impressions.

STATISTICAL RESULTS

YEAR	TOTAL	PER CAPITA
1850	$7,135,780,228	308
1860	16,159,616,068	514
1870	30,068,518,507	780
1880	43,642,000,000	870
1890	65,037,091,197	1,036

Somewhat more reliable evidence in this connection is afforded by the total production of cereals. There has been a very great increase in the per capita number of bushels, notwithstanding the fact that the proportion of the population engaged in agriculture has declined, leaving more people to devote themselves to satisfying other wants of society than those for food.

PRODUCTION OF CEREALS IN BUSHELS

YEAR	TOTAL [2]	PER CAPITA
1849	871,042,524	37.5
1859	1,242,159,398	39.5
1869	1,388,526,403	34.8
1879	2,699,415,752	53.8
1889	3,520,960,086	56.2
1899	4,434,698,746	58.6

[1] Eleventh Census, 1890, " Wealth, Debt and Taxation," Pt. II, p. 14. The census figures for 1900 are not yet printed, but Colonel Carroll D. Wright, in an article in the *Independent* for May 1, 1902, makes an estimate for 1900 of $94,000,000,000, which would give a per capita wealth of $1,244.

[2] Census of 1900, " Agriculture," Pt. II, p. 16.

The following table will show the decline in the proportion of people engaged in agriculture, and the corresponding increase in other lines of work:[1] —

CLASSES OF OCCUPATIONS	PER CENT		
	1900	1890	1880
	Mainland		
Agriculture	35.7	37.7	44.3
Professional Service . . .	4.3	4.1	3.5
Domestic and Personal Service .	19.2	18.6	19.7
Trade and Transportation . .	16.4	14.6	10.7
Manufactures and Mechanical Ind.	24.4	25.0	21.8
Total	100.0	100.0	100.0

In 1880 the proportion engaged in agriculture was considerably greater than the proportion engaged in the last two groups of occupations, but in 1900 the reverse was true.

That we have become to an increasing extent a manufacturing nation is of course a commonplace. The following general table from the Census of 1900 tells a clear story, although the reader is warned against using the figures for other purposes than to show a general progress. It would lead to error, for example, to compare the per capita value of products here given with average wages, since the value of products is a gross value, containing many reduplications.

[1] Twelfth Census, "Population," Pt. II, p. cxxxiii.

STATISTICAL RESULTS

COMPARATIVE SUMMARY, 1850–1890 [1]

	1900	1890	1880
Number of Establishments	512,339	355,415	253,852
Capital	9,835,086,909	6,525,156,486	2,790,272,606
Total Wages . . .	2,328,691,254	1,891,228,321	947,953,795
Cost of Materials .	7,348,144,755	5,162,044,076	3,396,823,549
Value of Products, including custom work and repairing	13,014,287,498	9,372,437,283	5,369,579,191

	1870	1860	1850
Number of Establishments	252,148	140,433	123,025
Capital	2,118,208,769	1,009,855,715	533,245,351
Total Wages . . .	775,584,343	378,878,966	236,755,464
Cost of Materials .	2,488,427,242	1,031,605,092	555,123,822
Value of Products, including custom work and repairing	4,232,325,442	1,885,861,676	1,019,106,616

The value of products increased about thirteen times from 1850 to 1900, but in the same period the population increased only from three to four times.

It is of interest to compare the relative importance of the great groups of industries contributing to this total product. Food and kindred products, iron and steel and their products, textiles, and lumber and its remanufactures constitute one-half the total product : —

[1] Twelfth Census, " Manufactures," Pt. I, p. xlvii.

Groups of Industries [1]	Number of Establishments	Value of Product
Food and kindred products . .	61,302	$2,277,702,010
Textiles	30,048	1,637,484,484
Iron and steel and their products	13,896	1,793,490,908
Lumber and its remanufactures .	47,079	1,030,906,579
Leather and its finished products	16,989	583,731,046
Paper and printing	26,747	606,317,768
Liquors and beverages . . .	7,861	425,504,167
Chemicals and allied products .	5,444	552,891,877
Clay, glass, and stone products .	14,809	293,564,235
Metals and metal products other than iron and steel . . .	16,305	748,795,464
Tobacco	15,252	283,076,546
Vehicles for land transportation .	10,113	508,649,129
Shipbuilding	1,116	74,578,158
Miscellaneous industries . . .	29,479	1,004,092,294
Hand trades	215,814	1,183,615,478
All Industries	512,254	13,004,400,143

The use of steam is one of the things that has made possible this great industrial development. The extent to which water power has been replaced by steam and other power is shown in the following table: —

PER CENT THAT STEAM, WATER, AND OTHER POWER IS OF THE TOTAL HORSE-POWER IN THE UNITED STATES [2]

Year	Steam	Water	Other Power
1870	51.8	48.2	
1880	64.1	35.9	
1890	78.3	21.2	0.5
1900	77.4	15.3	7.3

[1] Twelfth Census, " Manufactures," Pt. I, p. lxvi.

[2] *Ibid.*, p. cccxxxviii.

STATISTICAL RESULTS

In the census of 1900 statistics were gathered concerning industrial combinations, but the following paragraph from the report of the Industrial Commission will give a better idea of the extent of the trust movement than any figures we can give : —

" The census figures do not permit a comparison of the proportion of any particular industry which is controlled by industrial combinations, and therefore give no clew to the extent to which such combinations are able to monopolize any industry. In many of the most important lines of industry combinations have secured control of a large percentage of the country's production. In many articles of steel a single combination controls 75 to 80 per cent of the output, and in some lines even more; in sugar, about 90 per cent ; in petroleum, at least 82 per cent. In other industries, although the percentage of the entire output controlled by combinations is not so large, still there are organizations with very large capital. In the raising or distribution of agricultural products, such combinations, though not unknown — *e.g.* the United Fruit Company — are still rare. While a beginning has been made toward the combination of mercantile industries, not merely in department stores, but also in the union of several large establishments along similar lines, such as the combination organized by H. B. Claflin, yet by far the largest proportion of our mercantile business is still owned and managed by relatively small concerns. Many manufacturing industries, such as clothing, dressmaking, millinery, small tools, electrical specialties, house-furnishing materials, the textiles, and numerous other articles are substantially free from large combinations. The manufacture of cotton is perhaps the most important in which no combination of large size exists." [1]

In spite of the fact that we have been becoming an industrial nation, the leading items of our exports are still agricultural products, as is shown by the following table : —

THE TEN LEADING ARTICLES OF EXPORT IN THE YEAR
ENDING JUNE 1, 1901 [2]

	PER CENT OF TOTAL EXPORTS
1. Cotton, unmanufactured	21.48
2. Breadstuffs	18.87
3. Provisions, comprising meats and dairy products .	13.49
4. Iron and steel, and manufactures of . . .	8.03
5. Mineral oils	4.87
6. Wood, and manufactures of	3.59
7. Animals	3.57
8. Copper, and manufactures of	3.05
9. Tobacco, and manufactures of	2.24
10. Leather, and manufactures of	1.91

[1] Report of the Industrial Commission, Vol. XIX, p. 604.

[2] Annual Report of Treasury Department on Foreign Commerce and Navigation of the United States for year ending June 1, 1901, Vol. I, p. 164.

Cotton, breadstuffs, and provisions still make up over one-half of our exports. It will be of interest to compare with the foregoing a list of the —

TEN LEADING ARTICLES OF IMPORT IN THE YEAR ENDING
JUNE 1, 1901 [1]

	PER CENT OF TOTAL IMPORTS
1. Sugar	10.99
2. Coffee	7.64
3. Chemicals, drugs, and dyes	6.50
4. Hides and skins	5.86
5. Cotton, manufactures of	4.89
6. Fibre, vegetable, etc., manufactures of . .	3.98
7. Silk, unmanufactured	3.65
8. India rubber and gutta percha, crude . . .	3.50
9. Silk, manufactures of	3.26
10. Fibres, vegetables, etc., unmanufactured . .	2.79

These ten articles amounted to 53 per cent of the total imports in the year 1901. The imports of the United States are chiefly food and raw products, but manufactured articles are still a large although a declining part of them. In 1890, luxuries, manufactures ready for consumption, and manufactured articles for use as materials in mechanic arts constituted 44 per cent of the total imports, but in 1901 only 40 per cent.[2]

[1] Annual Report of Treasury Department on Foreign Commerce and Navigation of the United States for year ending June 1, 1901, Vol. I, p. 100.

[2] See Report of Industrial Commission, Vol. XIX, pp. 556–558.

EVOLUTION OF INDUSTRIAL SOCIETY

The following table shows the growth in our commerce since 1790: —

COMMERCE OF 1901 COMPARED WITH AVERAGE OF DECENNIAL PERIODS, 1790–1900 [1]

TEN-YEAR PERIODS	ANNUAL AVERAGE OF TEN-YEAR PERIODS OF —	
	Imports	Exports
1790–1800	$59,184,545	$46,774,236
1801–1810	92,766,351	74,531,506
1811–1820	80,811,927	58,989,222
1821–1830	72,948,879	69,431,024
1831–1840	119,520,679	103,550,201
1841–1850	118,094,779	119,554,936
1851–1860	284,475,036	248,887,460
1861–1870	331,867,029	254,326,410
1871–1880	535,221,512	589,300,719
1881–1890	692,186,522	765,135,498
1891–1900	763,327,858	1,024,869,210
1901 (Fiscal Year) . .	823,172,165	1,487,764,991

We see here a remarkable growth in the excess of exports over imports. It is not clear just how the international account is being balanced. Foreign nations cannot, of course, make good the balance by continued shipments in gold. It doubtless is true that, to some extent, we are becoming a creditor nation, or at any rate, ceasing to be a debtor nation.

[1] Annual Report of Treasury Department on Foreign Commerce and Navigation, 1901, Vol. I, p. 19.

STATISTICAL RESULTS

One of the clearest evidences of the internal growth of industry that statistics offer is in the increase every decade in the number of miles of railways in operation : [1]—

Year	Miles	Year	Miles
1830 . . .	23	1880 . . .	93,262
1840 . . .	2,818	1890 . . .	166,654
1850 . . .	9,021	1900 . . .	194,334
1860 . . .	30,626	1901 . . .	198,787
1870 . . .	52,922		

In thinking of the benefits which the development of a great transportation system has brought, we should not forget at what a cost of human life it is being operated. The following is the record for the last five years : —

RAILROAD ACCIDENTS IN THE UNITED STATES [2]

Year	Employees		Passengers		Other Persons		Total	
	Killed	Injured	Killed	Injured	Killed	Injured	Killed	Injured
1897	1,693	27,667	222	2,795	4,522	6,269	6,437	36,731
1898	1,958	31,761	221	2,945	4,680	6,176	6,859	40,882
1899	2,210	34,923	239	3,442	4,674	6,255	7,123	44,620
1900	2,550	39,643	249	4,128	5,066	6,549	7,865	50,320
1901	2,675	41,142	282	4,988	5,498	7,209	8,455	53,339

[1] Taken from Poore's " Manual of Railroads," 1902, p. v.

[2] Report of the Interstate Commerce Commission, " Statistics of Railroads," 1901, p. 97.

Just to what extent the increased production of wealth has been shared in by all classes, statistics do not tell us very clearly. There is good reason to believe that, absolutely, wages have been rising, even though the worker may possibly not have been getting his full share of increased production. Prices have been steadily falling, and yet money wages have on the whole risen. The following table will be of interest in this connection : —

MOVEMENT OF AVERAGE DAILY WAGES[1] IN GOLD IN CERTAIN CITIES OF THE UNITED STATES (REPRESENTING 255 QUOTATIONS) AND OF PRICES[2] IN GOLD

YEAR	WAGES	PRICE INDEX	YEAR	WAGES	PRICE INDEX
1870 . .	2.20\frac{1}{2}$	119.0	1884 . .	$2.49	102.6
1871 . .	2.39$\frac{1}{4}$	122.9	1885 . .	2.47$\frac{1}{4}$	93.3
1872 . .	2.45	121.4	1886 . .	2.47$\frac{1}{4}$	93.4
1873 . .	2.35$\frac{1}{2}$	114.5	1887 . .	2.49$\frac{1}{4}$	94.5
1874 . .	2.30$\frac{1}{4}$	116.6	1888 . .	2.50$\frac{3}{4}$	96.2
1875 . .	2.24$\frac{1}{4}$	114.6	1889 . .	2.51$\frac{1}{2}$	98.5
1876 . .	2.18	108.7	1890 . .	2.52$\frac{3}{4}$	93.7
1877 . .	2.24$\frac{1}{2}$	107.0	1891 . .	2.54$\frac{1}{2}$	94.4
1878 . .	2.30$\frac{3}{4}$	103.2	1892 . .	2.56	
1879 . .	2.32	95.0	1893 . .	2.54$\frac{1}{4}$	
1880 . .	2.34	104.9	1894 . .	2.49$\frac{1}{4}$	
1881 . .	2.40$\frac{3}{4}$	108.4	1895 . .	2.47$\frac{1}{4}$	
1882 . .	2.44$\frac{3}{4}$	109.1	1896 . .	2.45$\frac{3}{4}$	
1883 . .	2.47	106.6	1897 . .	2.44$\frac{1}{2}$	
			1898 . .	2.43$\frac{1}{4}$	

[1] Bulletin Department of Labor, 1898, p. 668.

[2] Aldrich Report, "Wholesale Prices, Wages, and Transportation," Washington, 1893, Pt. I, p. 100. The Aldrich Report receives

STATISTICAL RESULTS

Later investigations give the following results for the years succeeding 1890 : —

Year	Relative Wages [1]	Relative Prices [2]
1890		112.9
1891	100	111.7
1892	100.30	106.1
1893	99.32	105.6
1894	98.06	96.1
1895	97.88	93.6
1896	97.93	90.4
1897	98.96	89.7
1898	98.79	93.4
1899	101.54	101.7
1900	103.43	110.5
1901		108.5

The first column includes data pertaining to 148 establishments, representing 26 industries and 192 occupations. The year 1891 is taken as a base for wages with which to compare the other years.

The second column is the summary of the relative prices of 261 commodities, the average price for 1890–1899 being taken as the base.

Whatever increase in wages there has been, it should be partly attributed to the efforts of trade

searching criticism from Professor Charles J. Bullock in his paper, "Contributions to the History of Wage Statistics," which appeared in the quarterly publications of the American Statistical Association, March, 1899, Vol. VI.

[1] Bulletin Department of Labor, 1900, p. 914.

[2] *Ibid.*, March, 1902, p. 235.

unions. Workers have had to fight for the increase. From the following figures we see that, in twenty-one years, the strikes in slightly over a half the establishments succeeded, in about a third they failed, and in the rest succeeded partly:[1]—

YEAR	PER CENT OF ESTABLISHMENTS IN WHICH STRIKES		
	Succeeded	Succeeded partly	Failed
1881	61.37	7.00	31.63
1882	53.59	8.17	38.24
1883	58.17	16.09	25.74
1884	51.50	3.89	44.61
1885	52.80	9.50	37.70
1886	34.50	18.85	46.65
1887	45.64	7.19	47.17
1888	52.22	5.48	42.30
1889	46.49	18.91	34.60
1890	52.65	10.01	37.34
1891	37.88	8.29	53.83
1892	39.31	8.70	51.99
1893	50.86	10.32	38.82
1894	38.09	13.50	48.41
1895	55.24	9.94	34.82
1896	59.19	7.47	33.34
1897	57.31	28.12	14.57
1898	64.19	6.38	29.43
1899	73.24	14.25	12.51
1900	46.43	20.62	32.95
TOTAL	50.77	13.04	36.19

[1] Sixteenth Annual Report of the Commissioner of Labor, 1901, p. 35.

Somewhat less favorable results are shown when the percentage which the successful strikers constitute of the whole number of persons engaged is considered.

Another way in which the working classes are being benefited is in the efforts that have been made to restrict child labor in factories. It is instructive to compare the movement in the various geographical divisions. In the cotton manufacture, for example, there is a marked decline in all sections except in the Southern states : —

THE COTTON MANUFACTURE [1]

Percentage of Wage-earners who are Children under 16 years of age, 1870–1900

GEOGRAPHICAL DIVISIONS	1870	1880	1890	1900
New England states . . .	14.5	13.9	6.9	6.7
Middle states	22.0	21.2	12.6	12.0
Southern states	23.0	24.5	24.2	25.1
Western states	31.1	21.3	13.2	9.0
United States	17.0	16.2	10.7	13.3

A decline in the death-rate is a reliable indication of better conditions of living. Improvements in the water supply and sanitary regulations of many kinds make for well-being in ways that do not admit of money measurement. That progress has recently been made in this direction is evident from the following figures, showing the death-rate in 1880 and 1890 in certain cities : —

[1] Census of 1900, " Manufactures," Pt. I, p. cxxviii.

CITIES	DEATH-RATE	
	1900	1890
Albany, N.Y.	19.3	25.5
Auburn, N.Y.	17.2	22.1
Boston, Mass.	20.1	23.4
Brockton, Mass.	13.2	15.2
Brooklyn, N.Y.	19.9	24.0
Buffalo, N.Y.	14.8	18.4
Chelsea, Mass.	18.7	20.2
Cincinnati, Ohio	19.1	21.0
Cleveland, Ohio	17.1	20.2
Hartford, Conn.	19.4	24.4
Jersey City, N.J.	20.7	25.6
Lawrence, Mass.	20.2	27.8
Lowell, Mass.	19.8	25.9
Newark, N.J.	19.8	27.4
New Haven, Conn.	17.2	18.8
New York, N.Y.	21.3	26.7
North Adams, Mass.	13.8	20.3
Rochester, N.Y.	15.0	17.3
Schenectady, N.Y.	15.1	22.2
Taunton, Mass.	19.8	21.7
Washington, D.C.	22.8	23.7
Yonkers, N.Y.	16.3	17.1

It is instructive to compare the changes in the death-rate at different age periods. The chief reduction of the death-rate has been in the earlier ages, and this means that a larger proportion of those born survive to the non-dependent or useful ages.[2] The following table shows that

[1] Twelfth Census, "Vital Statistics," Pt. I, p. lxi.

[2] Newsholme, "Vital Statistics," 3d ed., London, 1899, p. 304.

the expectation of life at these ages has increased : [1]—

		ENGLAND AND WALES		
		1838-1854	1871-1880	1881-1890
Average lifetime between 16 and 65 years of age	Males	25.86	27.09	28.97
	Females	26.86	29.01	30.99

While this table is for England and Wales, the decline in the death-rate would indicate similar results in the United States. Furthermore, it is to be observed that in sanitary measures and in what is called " public medicine," we have as yet scarcely made more than a beginning. We have reason to anticipate further progress and an increasing proportion of population in years of full vigor, the birth-rate declining somewhat, but a larger relative number surviving. This would seem to confirm the position that in the modern nation we have an increasing average of vigor and economic efficiency.

LITERATURE

Industrial history is a large subject on which a great deal has been written in recent years. The following references are to those more important works which are at the same time accessible without great difficulty. They should be in every public

[1] Newsholme, " Vital Statistics," 3d ed., London, 1899, p. 309.

library of any importance. The references in the foot-notes will be helpful to those who wish to make a special study of the subject.

ASHLEY, W. J., An Introduction to English Economic History and Theory. 2 vols. London and New York, 1888 and 1892. This is a scholarly work which traces the industrial evolution from the manor and the village community in the eleventh century to the close of the Middle Ages.

    Surveys Historic and Economic. London and New York, 1900. This work is valuable to the scholar on account of its reviews of works within the field of economic history.

BRUCE, P. H., Economic History of Virginia in the Seventeenth Century. 2 vols. New York, 1896.

BÜCHER, CARL, Industrial Evolution, translated from the German by S. Morley Wickett. New York, 1901. The author is Professor of Political Economy, University of Leipzig, and bases his popularly written, but scientific, work upon a wide survey of sources, particularly those which relate to primitive economic conditions. He has made additions to our knowledge, but exaggerates the difference between himself and earlier students of industrial history.

CHEYNEY, EDWARD P., An Introduction to the Industrial and Social History of England. New York, 1901. One of the best text-books on the subject.

CUNNINGHAM, WILLIAM, Growth of English Industry and Commerce. 2 vols. New York, 1890 and 1892. A work for scholars rather than the general reader.

CUNNINGHAM, WILLIAM, and MCARTHUR, ELLEN A., Outlines of English Economic and Industrial History. New York, 1898. This is written with fulness of knowledge, and is a brief but excellent text-book.

HOBSON, JOHN A., The Evolution of Modern Capitalism. New York, 1895. This work, which is scholarly, notwithstanding a few minor errors, is perhaps the most interesting of all the works on industrial history. It takes hold of the problems of our time in a more vital way than any of the other books. It is to be hoped that it will be revised and brought down to date, so as to give an account of the most recent developments.

MORGAN, LEWIS H., Ancient Society. New York, 1878. This work may be called a classic. It traces the evolution of society from savagery through barbarism to civilization. Since it was written a great deal of work has been done in this field, but Morgan still holds a high rank. A work for the scholar.

RAND, BENJAMIN, Selections illustrating Economic History since the Seven Years' War. Cambridge, 1892. This work contains reprints of the writings of others describing the most important events in economic history since 1763, and also includes transcripts of sections of the English and American Navigation Acts. It is valuable because it gives information, not easily accessible elsewhere, concerning the important events of this period.

TOYNBEE, ARNOLD, Industrial Revolution. London, 1884. A fragmentary but stimulating work.

WEEDEN, W. B., Economic and Social History of New England. 2 vols. Boston and New York, 1891.

WELLS, DAVID A., Recent Economic Changes. New York, 1889.

WRIGHT, CARROLL D., Industrial Evolution of the United States. New York, 1902.

PART II

SOME SPECIAL PROBLEMS OF INDUSTRIAL EVOLUTION

SOME SPECIAL PROBLEMS OF INDUSTRIAL EVOLUTION

CHAPTER I

COMPETITION: ITS NATURE, ITS PERMANENCY, AND ITS BENEFICENCE

A STRANGE contrast is afforded by the various utterances of popular economic literature touching the subject of competition. The following quotation furnishes us with a forceful expression of opinion adverse to competition, and may be taken as typical of views held by a class of sincere, enthusiastic champions of social reform : —

"Competition is not law, but lawlessness. Carried to its logical outcome it is anarchy or the absence of law. Man is a moral, spiritual, and social being, not dominated by animal law. There can be no such thing as a harmonized society with any competitive elements in it, and Christianity is impossible. Every man owes the world his life, and must live to have a life to give. In competitive conditions, not character, but cunning, survives. The gospel of success is the great insanity of modern materialism, absorbing the best brain, thought, and life of the race ; we have been feeding our children to this great Moloch of success, but as a result we have been warping the intellect and making moral idiots.

"We are coming to a higher evolution, in which the law of mutual service shall be the law of life. Any attempt to build society on a competitive foundation is fundamentally anarchical. The idea of brotherhood has come to stay, and will not back down at the bidding of politicians, monopolists, or theologians. The years behind us are but a getting together of human material in a divine effort of perfected humanity. Democracy must be applied to reorganizing the machinery of the world." [1]

Now let us put over against this utterance a clear-cut expression of opinion as favorable to competition as the words we have just used are unfavorable to this manifestation of social force in our economic life : —

"Competition was the gigantic motor that caused nearly everybody during the first nineteen centuries of Christian civilization to use all his mental and physical powers to get ahead. The best efforts of humanity, stimulated by competition . . . have lifted our race to a standard where the mode of living of common laborers is more comfortable and desirable than the everyday existence of the kings of whom Homer sings." [2]

---

[1] Cleveland *Citizen*, March 14, 1896. Attributed to George D. Herron.

[2] Richard Michaelis in " Looking Further Forward," pp. v and 85.

Once again listen to this vigorous outburst in denunciation of competition, written some fifty years ago by a distinguished leader of Christian socialism in England : " Sweet competition ! Heavenly maid ! . . . Nowadays hymned alike by penny-a-liners and philosophers as the ground of all society, . . . the only real preserver of the earth ! Why not of Heaven, too ? Perhaps there is competition among the angels, and Gabriel and Raphael have won their rank by doing the maximum of worship on the minimum of grace. We shall know some day. In the meanwhile, 'these are thy works, thou parent of all good!' Man eating man, man eaten by man, in every variety of degree and method ! Why does not some enthusiastic political economist write an epic on 'The Consecration of Cannibalism'?"[1]

On the other hand, listen to these words by a sturdy American, whcse courage in denunciation of wrong in high places no one can rightly impugn : —

"The competition of economics is not the so-called competition of our great centres, where men strive to drive men to the wall, but the competition which leaves each in full possession of that productive power which best unites his labor with the labor of others. Competition is no more trespass than it is theft. It is the reconciliation of men in those productive processes which issue in the larg-

[1] Charles Kingsley, in "Cheap Clothes and Nasty," printed with Alton Locke, Vol. I, pp. 82–83.

est aggregate of wealth. It is not crowding men off their feet, but a means of planting them upon their feet." [1]

These quotations could be multiplied indefinitely on the one side and on the other. We find it asserted on the one hand that competition is sinful warfare; that it is "division, disunion, every man for himself, every man against his brother";[2] on the other hand that it is mutual service; that it is altruism of a superior quality; that it is the essence of the golden rule; that it is loving our neighbor as ourselves—in other words, that a correct rendering of Christian love is competition.[3]

Apparently such contradictory views admit of no reconciliation. But when we think seriously about the matter, we are forced to ask ourselves the question: How is it possible that men of undoubted capacity, of unquestioned sincerity, of warm enthusiasm for humanity, can hold views respecting competition, this great corner-stone of our economic order, so diametrically opposed that what the one cordially hates the other ardently admires as a source of abundance for all the deserving children of men? May it not be that, after all, these disputants are talking about somewhat different things, and that what is needed, first of all, is definition?

---

[1] John Bascom, on the "Moral Discipline of Business," *The Kingdom*, Minneapolis, May, 1896.   [2] Kingsley, *loc. cit.*, p. 104.

[3] Edward Atkinson, on "Coöperative Competition," *The New World*, September, 1895.

What, precisely, do we have in mind when we discuss competition? Competition, in a large sense, means a struggle of conflicting interests. If we open our dictionaries and read the definitions there given, we shall find something like this in each one of them, " The act of seeking or endeavoring to gain what another is endeavoring to gain at the same time; common contest, or striving for the same object; strife for superiority; rivalry " ("Century Dictionary ").

Professor Gide uses these words to tell us what he understands by competition in this large sense, " When each individual in a country is at liberty to take the action he considers the most advantageous for himself, whether as regards the choice of an employment or the disposal of his goods, we are living under the régime of competition." [1]

But we do not have enough precision in these definitions to answer our purposes. Economic competition, it is true, is a struggle of conflicting interests for valuable things, for what we call, in its widest sense, wealth. But is all struggle for wealth competition? If I knock you down with a sand-bag and rob you, is that to be called competition? If I fit out an armed ship and prey upon the commerce of the world, is that competition? If I cheat you by a lie, are the lie and the fraud part of the competitive process? The reply comes

---

[1] " Principles of Political Economy," by Charles Gide, translated by E. P. Jacobsen, 1892, p. 64.

naturally, " No, you are now talking about criminal and wrong action."

But if it is not every struggle of conflicting interests that is to be denominated competition, we see at once that competition is a struggle which has its metes and bounds. I think we must say that the competitive struggle is limited by constitutional and statute law. It is a struggle whose boundaries are fixed by the social order within the framework of which we live and move and exercise our faculties in the pursuit of a livelihood. When we bear this qualification in mind, simple and obvious as it is, many difficulties begin to vanish like fog before the rising sun. Many a man, when competition is mentioned, thinks of wild beasts, tearing and rending each other in a death struggle for an insufficient supply of food. But such is only an incomplete and imperfect picture of the struggle for life, even among the brutes, and does not at all describe the struggle of competition among civilized men.

But even when we call to mind the limitations placed upon the struggle of conflicting economic interests by the social order, we do not yet have a sufficient idea of economic competition. It is essential that we add another element to our idea, in order to render it more nearly conformable to reality. We must bring to mind the great principle of evolution which is present wherever there is life. Nothing could well be more unscientific in the present age of science than to leave evolution out of account in our examination of anything so fundamental in society as competition. What light, then, does the principle of evolution throw upon competition?

The struggle for existence among the lower animals has become a commonplace of modern scientific thought, and equally familiar are the selective processes of nature, resulting in the survival of those fittest for their environment at a particular time and place. Not quite so familiar to all are other aspects of nature's methods. After the appearance of Darwin's epoch-making book, " The Origin of Species," biologists first brought out the hard and cruel side of the struggle for existence. Rousseau's pictures of mild and beneficent nature were replaced in their descriptions by the conception of nature as " red in tooth and claw with ravin." Even Huxley spoke of the animal world as on about the same level as a gladiator's show. " The creatures," said he, " are fairly well treated and set to fight ; whereby the strongest, the swiftest, the cunningest, live to fight another day. The spectator has no need to turn his thumb down, as no quarter is given." [1]

Huxley in the words just quoted, is discussing the cruelty with which nature treats the lower animals. When he came to discuss 'the relation of man to nature, he found the process of external physical nature equally — or even more — cruel, and

[1] " The Struggle for Existence," *Nineteenth Century*, February, 1888.

saw the only method of escape in the introduction of a human principle opposed to nature. This nature-process he speaks of as cosmic, and in his opinion this cosmic process is greatest in the most rudimentary stages and declines as civilization advances. "Social Progress," he says, "means a checking of the cosmic process at every step, and the substitution for it of another, which may be called the ethical process; the end of which is not the survival of those who may happen to be the fittest, in respect to the whole of the conditions which exist, but of those who are ethically the best." [1]

Later biological researches have seemed to make nature's competitive process still more cruel. Herbert Spencer has long been the most prominent leader among those who have followed Lamarck in the doctrine that acquired qualities can be transmitted. This doctrine Spencer has developed in its social aspects. It is a cheerful, optimistic doctrine for the human race. It means that the improvements which men acquire by their various physical and mental educational processes, accumulated in their own persons, can be transmitted to their offspring, and so to successive generations, and continuous improvement may take place in the qualities of those who are born. We have, or at any rate we may have, according to this doctrine, an increasing stock of qualities acquired and trans-

[1] *Vide* Huxley's "Evolution and Ethics," the Romanes Lecture of 1893, p. 33.

mitted. Professor August Weismann has, however, in recent years been a leader among those who have disputed this doctrine, maintaining that the qualities which are acquired during lifetime are not transmitted to offspring, and, consequently, that the efforts of parents to improve themselves do not benefit their children by means of physical heredity. To use one of a thousand illustrations, all the efforts of a parent to improve himself musically do not make it one whit the easier for the child to become a musician. This doctrine is held to, in the main, still by biologists, although we have now a school of Neo-Lamarckians, who think that, within certain limits, acquired characteristics and qualities can be transmitted to offspring by physical heredity. Weismannism means that it is only by a weeding-out process, through selection, that physical improvement is to take place. The apparent cruelty of this selective weeding-out process has found frequent expression. Professor Lester F. Ward says that if Weismannism is true, then "education has no value for the future of mankind, and its benefits are confined exclusively to the generation receiving it." [1] And Professor Le Conte uses the following language: "If it be true that reason must direct the course of human evolution, and if it be also true that selection of the fittest is the only method available for that purpose; then, if we are to have any race improvement

[1] Quoted by Alfred Russel Wallace in "Studies, Scientific and Social," Vol. II, p. 508.

at all, the dreadful law of the destruction of the weak and helpless must, with Spartan firmness, be carried out voluntarily and deliberately. Against such a course, all that is best in us revolts." [1] Mr. Benjamin Kidd, in his well-known work, "Social Evolution," attempted a sociological treatment of Weismannism. According to him, there is a necessary antagonism between the interests of the individual and the interests of society as a whole. He claims that the progress of the race results from a growth of population, which is excessive when we regard it from the standpoint of the interest of the individual. The excessive population must lead to the rejection of the inferior members of society, allowing the superior alone to live, and to continue the race. The unfit must become extinct. It is the office of religion, according to this theory, to induce the individual to follow a line of conduct which is antagonistic to his own interests, and for which reason affords no sanction. Religion, then, has as its function, to induce the individual to submit to the sacrifice of his interests for the sake of the whole, and to afford him consolation while he is doing so. We reach in this development the logical outcome of one line of thought-evolution.

But it was not long before careful observation revealed other aspects of nature's processes. Mr. Alfred Russel Wallace long ago called attention to

[1] Quoted by Alfred Russel Wallace in "Studies, Scientific and Social," Vol. II, p. 508.

the comparatively painless character of the struggle among animals, and to the large amount of happiness in their lives. After reviewing the ethical aspect of the struggle for existence, he expressed the opinion that it affords "the maximum of life and of the enjoyment of life with the minimum of suffering and pain."[1] When we watch animal existences as a whole, and not in exceptional moments, can we conclude otherwise? But subsequent observers, going farther, have called attention first to the fact that the struggle is not for life merely, but for the life of others. These others are first of all offspring, but later mates and companions. Again, attention has been called to association and mutual aid among animals as part of the struggle for existence, and we have come to see that coöperation and the ability to coöperate are powerful weapons, even in the competitive subhuman struggle for existence.[2]

[1] " Darwinism," p. 40.

[2] Consult the series of articles on " Mutual Aid " by P. Kropotkin in the *Nineteenth Century*, September and November, 1890, April, 1891, and January, 1892, August and September, 1894, January and June, 1896.

These articles with a few additions have been published in book form under the title " Mutual Aid a Factor of Evolution." Mutual aid is traced by Kropotkin continuously from the lower animals to human beings. A distinction must be made, however, and a radical one. Among the lower animals mutual aid is a biological fact, which is a result of increased efficiency in the struggle for existence either with other animals or the physical environment, that is, the obstacles to existence in nature. This is different from the conscious coöperation of men in their higher activities.

We must hasten on to the point where, as a result of organic evolution, we have the emergence of man. Among primitive men competition seems at first to take on more cruel forms than among animals.[1] But if evolution has apparently gone back a few steps, it is only to move forward mightily and unceasingly as social evolution for the achievement of ends whose grandeur we as yet but faintly apprehend. Competition, begun far below man with the very beginnings of life, persists as one of the most fundamental laws of animate existence, but evolution carries it to higher and ever higher planes. Primitive competition includes a narrow circle of association and, beyond that, slaughter for economic advantage. With social evolution slaughter gradually recedes into the background and falls below competition into the region of crime.[2] When men considered it dishonorable to gain by the sweat of the brow what could be won by the sword, battle belonged to economic competition; not so in the age of industry. From early times, and until recently, the competitive social order found within its framework a place for slavery; but as a result of social evolution, continued for ages, slavery falls below the plane of competition and is now regarded as

[1] See Darwin's " Descent of Man," Pt. III, Ch. XXI, where he compares favorably a monkey and baboon with savages.

[2] Huxley says of civilized man that " in extreme cases he does his best to put an end to the survival of the fittest of former days by axe and rope." See " Evolution and Ethics," p. 6.

incompatible with civilization. Piracy, until a comparatively recent period of the world's history, held an honorable place within the competitive processes whereby men secured economic gain; but that in turn has fallen outside of and below the social order of competition.[1]

But since the beginning of this century, along with the persistence and increasing intensity of competition, elevation of the plane of competition has kept pace with the rapidity of social evolution. The labor of very young children has been outlawed; the labor even of grown men has in many cases been restricted, and unwholesome conditions and oppressive practices in numberless instances have been put below the plane of competition. We need not retrace this familiar ground. A former president of this Association, in one of its early publications[2] declared that one of the functions of government is to raise the ethical level of competition. He was himself surprised to find the

---

[1] Piracy and commerce were in primitive times very generally closely associated, and the former must be regarded as one of the chief origins of the latter. In the time of Homer the Phœnicians were both pirates and merchants. Where they had an opportunity by reason of superior strength to take goods from strangers, they did so without hesitation and apparently without the slightest moral scruples. Where, however, they came in contact with those too strong to be robbed, they appeared as traders and made profitable exchanges. "Phœnician" signified to the Greeks liar, thief, and kidnapper. See Keller's "Homeric Society," pp. 14–15.

[2] Henry C. Adams, "The Relation of the State to Industrial Action." Publications of the American Economic Association, Vol. I, No. 6, January, 1887, pp. 507–508.

impression that the phrase produced. It produced that profound impression precisely because it is so pregnant with meaning. The phrase is a key, opening mysteries and revealing reconciliations of science and humanity.

We have already mentioned the fact of association among animals for mutual aid. Social evolution among men reveals growing association along with competition. One essential feature of social evolution, in its bearing on competition, is the enlargement of the associated competitive group. Here again the temptation to trespass upon your patience is strong, but it must be resisted. Many an address could be occupied entirely with a discussion of the grouping of men within the competitive social order. Thus we early find voluntary, loosely formed groups of employers pursuing common purposes; and also groups of workingmen likewise seeking to promote common interests. Again we notice a permanent organization of labor on the one hand and of capital on the other. Then we discover political associations embracing within themselves an infinite variety of competitive groups; and these political associations themselves having competitive features extend from the small hamlet to the mighty nation.[1] But competition does not stand alone. With it are associated sympathy, benevolence, and public authority. More-

[1] On this point the reader may compare Tarde's " Social Laws," pp. 29–133, and Fairbanks' " Introduction to Sociology," pp. 221–264.

over, wisely directed humanitarianism strengthens each group, while ruthless selfishness among the members of the group gradually destroys power in competition.[1] The larger the competitive group, the wider becomes the sphere for generosity, the larger the safe scope of pity, and the milder may the competition become for the individual. Witness how the progress of modern nations in philanthropy attends growing efficiency in their economic struggles. International competition is a stern fact of our time. Is it not equally a fact that the most potent nations in this great dramatic world-wide struggle of interests are precisely those nations in which we find the highest individual and social development of altruism? Association and coöperation, the healing touch, benevolence, love, are all compatible with competition.

Fear has sometimes been expressed lest the humanitarian side of social evolution should lead to weakness and degeneration, and the world be

[1] Darwin saw this very clearly and attributed the social instincts, with all that they imply, to natural selection. Social instincts include protection, sympathy, and love as important elements, and the result is mutual protection and aid, giving a distinct advantage to groups having these traits over those not possessing them, or possessing them in less high degree. To use Darwin's own words: " Animals endowed with the social instincts take pleasure in one another's company, warn one another of danger, defend and aid one another in many ways. These instincts do not extend to all the individuals of the species, but only to those of the same community. As they are highly beneficial to the species, they have in all probability been acquired through natural selection." " Descent of Man," Pt. III, Ch. XXI.

converted into Goethe's vast hospital. Such apprehension, I believe, does not rest upon a critical analysis of the forces at work in modern civilization. It is true that benevolence, manifested in and through progress, may keep alive some weak individuals, who in a harsher age would have perished, and that these weak individuals may take part in the propagation of the species, eventually leaving behind an enfeebled progeny. But with all its mildness, civilization lessens unfit reproduction, and, upon the whole does so to an ever increasing extent. It puts the feeble-minded in asylums, and discourages the marriage of paupers; while in its new attitude toward the criminal classes it shows an increasing inclination to detain them until it receives evidence that their malady is cured.[1] Moreover, by sanitation and other measures, modern civilization increases the strength and vigor of those who do survive. Comparisons of civilized men with savages and

[1] It must not be supposed that it is intended to assert that this movement has gone far enough. A few years ago it was estimated that only ten per cent of the feeble-minded were put under custodial care. All of them must be thus treated before the demands of benevolence and competition can be fully harmonized. But the movement has begun and is gathering force. It receives the support of modern scientific charity, and those workers in the field of charity who have sounded the alarm concerning the effects in this particular of indiscriminate charity, are optimistic concerning the power of society to control the evil in question and secure rational elimination along the lines indicated. This subject is further treated in Pt. II, Ch. III, which deals with "Social Progress and Race Improvement."

with semi-civilized peoples, reveal the superiority of the former in physical vigor.[1] It is probable that never in the world's history have there been men and women whose average of efficient strength in the economic sphere was so great as that of the men and women who to-day inhabit Germany, England, and the United States of America.

Now, it is to be noticed that the selective processes which we are adopting in civilized society involve a decrease of pain and an increase of happiness in proportion as knowledge advances. The problem is to keep the most unfit from reproduction, and to encourage the reproduction of those who are really the superior members of society. When we take up the measures in detail which are recommended by wise men for the accomplishment of this purpose, we find that in the long run they increase the true happiness of the individual.[2]

Competition is the chief selective process in

[1] The following quotations from Bücher's "Industrial Evolution" confirm this view. "They [the Negritos in the Philippines] age early ; at forty or fifty the mountain Negritos are decrepit, white-haired bent old men." English translation, p. 9. "All the races involved in our survey . . . in bodily condition give the impression of backward, stunted growth. We are not on that account, however, justified in regarding them as degenerate race-fragments. The evidence rather goes to show that the more advanced races owe their higher physical development merely to the regular and more plentiful supply of food which agriculture and cattle-raising for centuries past have placed within their reach." Cf. Alfred Russel Wallace's "Studies Scientific and Social," Vol. II, pp. 494-497.

[2] This subject receives more detailed and careful treatment in the chapter on "Social Progress and Race Improvement."

modern economic society, and through it we have the survival of the fit. But what do we mean by "the fit"? We all know to-day that fitness has reference simply to conditions of a particular time and place. Bold and aggressive pirates were at one time fit for survival, but now they are likely to come to an untimely and ignominious end. Modern society itself establishes, consciously or unconsciously, many of the conditions of the struggle for existence, and it is for society to create such economic conditions that only desirable social qualities shall constitute eminent fitness for survival. A kind of society is possible, in which the beggar has this fitness, while the conditions in another society may be most unfavorable to the growth of parasitical classes.

The socially established competitive methods and the socially established ends to be attained by competition determine the kind of men who will survive in competition. Let me offer an illustration. To-day the civil service of the modern nation furnishes an opportunity for a livelihood to a considerable percentage of the population. Competition for admission to the civil service in order thereby to secure a support is found when we have the so-called spoils system, and the competition is intense and frequently bitter. This competitive contest issues in the survival of men with qualities known to us all. Civil-service reform does not remove competition; on the contrary it extends competition, but the difference in methods produces corresponding differences in results. On the one hand, the extension of competition lessens bitterness, because it is more in consonance with our ethical demand for equality of opportunity; and the difference in competitive tests for success, issues in the survival of men with qualities of another sort from those who come to the top under the spoils system, and with qualities, most of us will say, of a higher kind.

Competition increasingly comes to mean worthy struggle, and true progress implies that success will be secured hereafter by conformity to higher and ever higher, nobler and ever nobler ideals.

Mr. Alfred Russel Wallace and Professor Lester F. Ward have called attention to the superiority of man's selection to nature's selection. Professor Ward has thus expressed the idea: "The economics of nature consists, therefore, essentially in the operation of the law of competition in its purest form. The prevailing idea, however, that it is the fittest possible that survive in this struggle is wholly false. The effect of competition is to prevent any form from attaining its maximum development, and to maintain a comparatively low level for all forms that succeed in surviving. This is made clear by the fact that wherever competition is wholly removed, as through the agency of man, in the interest of any one form, that form immediately begins to make great strides and soon outstrips all those that depend upon competition. Such has been the case with all the cereals and fruit trees ; it is the case with domestic cattle and sheep, with horses, dogs, and all the forms of life that man has excepted from the biologic law and subjected to the law of mind ; and both the agricultural and the pastoral stages of society rest upon the successful resistance which rational man has offered to the law of nature in these departments. So that we have now to add to the waste of competition its influence in preventing the really fittest from surviving." [1]

While in general we must agree with Professor Ward, it is open to question whether or not the process which he describes is to be called the suppression of competition, for his language is apt to lead to erroneous conclusions on the part of most readers. We think of competition among men as a selective process, whereby men are favored and chosen for the fulfilment of social tasks. It is this selection which he apparently has in mind. Now, what man does by his culture of plants and animais is simply an improvement of unaided nature. He assists nature, and removes and destroys as completely and as rapidly as possible those species and individuals which are not adapted to his purposes, and then he makes the best possible environment for those which serve his purposes most fully. Man makes competition do its perfect work. Man establishes the environment and selects the plants and animals for survival in the prearranged environment. It may be well to

[1] " Outlines of Sociology," pp. 257–258.

repeat in different words what has already been said in regard to fitness, for the correct idea of fitness as a purely human idea cannot be too strongly emphasized. Weeds are just as fit for survival as the most nutritious food plant, so far as we can see when we have reference solely to external nature. Fitness means conformity to the conditions of the environment, and speaking from man's point of view it denotes both environment and survival suitable to human purposes. It is anthropo-teleological, to use a convenient technical term found frequently in Professor Ward's writings. Man makes an environment increasingly artificial as time goes on, and as he gains increasing power over the forces of nature.[1]

If the foregoing considerations are possessed of validity, we can readily see one of the tests to which we must submit proposed measures of social amelioration. A good social measure must strengthen the individual and the group for competition. On the other hand, the test of a bad condition is that it weakens individuals and groups, in the competitive struggle. Let me offer a single illustration.

In New York City a Tenement House Commission has been investigating the housing of the poorer classes in that city. Dr. Edward T. De-

---

[1] John Fiske has something very good on this in his "Destiny of Man," pp. 33–34, where he says, "Natural selection itself will by and by occupy a subordinate place in comparison with selection by man." But selection by man means regulated competition.

vine, Secretary of the Charity Organization Society of New York, testified before the Commission as follows: "There is much destitution directly due to overcrowding, to the lack of light and air, and to infected walls, ceilings, and floors. The experience of the agents and visitors of the Charity Organization Society confirms what physicians have said in regard to the danger from tuberculosis and other diseases. The chances of recovery are much less because of the lack of vitality due to the unfavorable physical conditions under which the people are obliged to live." [1] Here our test reveals a thoroughly bad competitive condition. But, on the other hand, Dr. Devine stated that, "While the Commission might not be able to devise laws that would directly lower rents, it would be possible to provide for greater decency and comfort, and for more of the conditions that make for life and health, without necessarily increasing rents." [2] We see in this last suggestion conformity to the tests of a desirable measure of social reform.

If our analysis is correct, it clearly follows that competition is a permanent feature of human society. It begins with the lowest orders of animals and continues its action among the highest orders of men. But it continually mounts to higher and higher elevations, and means rivalry

[1] *Charities*, the official organ of the Charity Organization Society of New York, December 1, 1900, p. 18.

[2] *Ibid.*, p. 19.

for ever better and better things.   We leave behind
contests for bare subsistence to engage in contests
for noble prizes of the mind and for opportunities
for social service.

We can, then, never allow competition to cease.
Combinations of labor and combinations of capital
may expand freely, so long as these combinations
mean merely association and coöperation.   But
when combinations mean monopoly, either competition must be restored or, where this is impossible,
the ends of competition must be secured by other
methods of social control; and if these methods
of social control in some cases mean public ownership and management of industries, a place must
be opened for the competitive principle in the
terms of admission to public employment.

It is at this point important to make a distinction
too often overlooked; namely, the radical difference between that socialistic extension of governmental activity which has in view the suppression
of competition, and that conservative demand for
an extension of governmental activity which has
in view the maintenance of competition.   There
are certain conditions of success in competition
which many economists believe cannot be supplied
individually, but must be furnished by collective
action.   Irrigation offers an illustration.   It appears
to be the general opinion of careful students of irrigation, that the laws of private property applied
to water used for purposes of irrigation, ultimately
produce cessation of competition; in other words,

monopoly; and that as a condition of permanent and wholesome competition along with associated efforts, large public activity is required in the supply of water. A recent writer uses these words, and, as I understand it, he simply voices the concensus of opinion among experts. "In the vast majority of instances, and over the larger portion of the arid region, costly works will be required, and these can only be supplied by some form of public enterprise. The dividends upon the investment must be looked for, not in the strong boxes of security-holders, but in the increase of national wealth, in social progress, and in economic gains." [1] If this statement is correct, we who believe in competition must, in order to secure the conditions of its maintenance, ask for larger governmental activity in matters of irrigation.

I regret that I can do no more here and now than merely to allude to two somewhat antagonistic lines of evolution. One is the movement which approaches — without hope of ever reaching — real equality of opportunities in economic competition. This is one of the most powerful movements of the century just drawing to a close and must be borne clearly in mind by any one who would understand the great historical movements of that century. The other line of development is found in the construction of great institutions which shut in and limit competition, but which

[1] William E. Smythe, on "The Struggle for Water in the West," *Atlantic Monthly*, November, 1900.

nevertheless are the very foundations upon which our civilization rests; the institutions which may be likened to social savings-banks or depositories of race achievements. I have here in mind the great economic-juridical institutions of society, such as private property, inheritance of property, and vested interests. The progressive approximation to equality in opportunities must not be permitted to go so far as to undermine these institutions. In the mutual adjustments of these two lines of evolution, namely, the equality-of-opportunity movement and the institutional movement, we have given us one of the weightiest and at the same time most delicate tasks of the twentieth century.

Competition thus conceived is beneficent, and the competitive order, rightly controlled by society, furnishes to men the maximum of pleasure with a minimum of pain. Not only does it insure progress for the race, but to an increasing extent all men participate in the benefits of this progress. We have no evidence that the competitive order is ultra-rational, and still less need we believe that it is anti-rational, as Mr. Kidd asserts.

Competition, suitably regulated, gives us a brave, strong race of men. Will they not use their bravery and strength for themselves exclusively? This question arises naturally, but the nature of the answer to it has already been intimated. We do not observe that weakness and cowardice are favorable to a considerate treatment of others;

bravery and strength make it relatively easy to be merciful; and there are ever in our civilized society forces at work which bend to the purposes of society bravery and strength. Social evolution accomplishes this result. It has been well said that as organic evolution gives us man, so social evolution gives the ideal man.[1] But economic competition is an essential constituent of that social evolution which is producing the ideal man;

[1] This thought finds beautiful expression in the following language of the late Professor Joseph Le Conte: " Organic evolution reached its term and completion in achieving man. But evolution did not stop there; for in achieving man it achieved also the possibility of another and higher kind of evolution, and was therefore transferred to a higher plane, and continued as social evolution or human progress. Now, as the highest end, the true significance, the *raison d'être* of organic evolution, was the achievement of man; so the highest and real meaning of society and social progress is the achievement of the ideal man. This view entirely changes the relation of the individual to society by giving a new and nobler meaning to society. Individual interests must be subordinated to social interests, not only because society is the greater organism, nor even because it represents all other individual interests; but also, and chiefly, because society is the only means of achieving the ideal. The higher law, from this point of view, is loyalty, not to society, as the ancients would have it, nor yet to the conscience, as we moderns would have it, but to the divine ideal of humanity. Fortunately for us, however, the highest interests of the individual are also thereby subserved. . . . But subordination is not sacrifice. On the contrary, it is the highest success for the individual. In subserving this, the highest interest of humanity, each individual is thereby subserving his own highest interests. In striving to advance the race toward the ideal, he is himself realizing that ideal in his own person." — " The Effect of the Theory of Evolution on Education." Proceedings of the National Educational Association, 1895.

and with competition are mingled other regulative principles. Psychologically, the ego and the alter ego, self and other self, arise together; economically they engage in many a conflict, but their spheres of interest are never entirely antagonistic to each other in the struggle for life. The ego — the self — enlarges the sphere of its selfhood ; and this widening and deepening goes on until the Christian ideal of humanity is at last attained.

But the upward struggle is part and parcel of the attainment of ideals; and, rightly conceived, elevated to a sufficient height, this struggle in economic life means competition ; it means rivalry in the service of self and other selves — rivalry in the upbuilding of the ideal man in the ideal society.

LITERATURE

While competition is mentioned in every systematic economic treatise, it has not received adequate scientific examination. Most economic writers have assumed the existence of competition without any critical examination of its nature and its workings, although certain hypotheses concerning it underlie all explanations of economic life in modern times. Somewhat more attention has been given by economists to competition in recent years, but it still remains for an economist to treat the subject exhaustively. The subject reaches beyond economics, and much of the best writing on it thus far has been done by those who are not professional economists. A few references which will prove helpful are given : —

BAKER, CHARLES WHITING, Monopolies and the People. 3d ed. New York, 1899. This work is especially note-worthy in this connection on account of Ch. X, pre-senting the Theory of Universal Competition, and Ch. XI, Laws of Modern Competition. This is one of the few attempts to define competition accurately and to formulate laws explaining its economic action. What has been done is scarcely more than a beginning, but as such it deserves more attention than it has received from economists.

BASCOM, JOHN, Social Theory, New York, 1895. Pt. II, Ch. II, Postulates of Economics.

CLARK, JOHN B., Distribution of Wealth. New York, 1899. This presents a theory of wages, interest, and profits as determined by competition working in an ideal manner. Many economists will be inclined to criticise the theory of competition here presented as altogether too opti-mistic. It must be remembered, however, that what is presented is not a picture of the actual world, but of the operation of competition in a world in which many restraints upon the workings of competition now existing are removed.

CLARK, JOHN B., and GIDDINGS, FRANKLIN H., The Modern Distributive Process. Boston, 1888. The first chapter of this book is upon the Limits of Competition, by Pro-fessor Clark, and the second upon the Persistence of Competition, by Professor Giddings. Even those not agreeing entirely with the positions taken by these two authors will admit that their treatment deserves careful consideration.

COOLEY, CHARLES H., Personal Competition. New York, 1899. This is one of the Economic Studies published by the American Economic Association. It is interest-ing and suggestive.

COMPETITION

Dictionary of Philosophy. Edited by J. MARK BALDWIN. New York, 1902. Articles, Competition; Existence, Struggle for; Rivalry.

FISKE, JOHN, The Destiny of Man, viewed in the Light of his Origin. Boston, 1884. Ch. XI, on the Universal Warfare of Primeval Man, and Ch. XII, First checked by the Beginnings of Industrial Civilization, have special significance in the study of competition. This subject finds further treatment in Mr. Fiske's more elaborate work, Outlines of Cosmic Philosophy, 2 vols., Boston, 1879; new edition with an introduction by Professor Josiah Royce, 4 vols., Boston, 1903.

HUXLEY, Struggle for Existence. Nineteenth Century, February, 1888.

KROPOTKIN, P., Mutual Aid a Factor of Evolution. New York, 1902.

MARSHALL, ALFRED, Some Aspects of Competition. Presidential address delivered to the Economic Science and Statistics Section of the British Association at Leeds, 1890. Published in the *Journal of the Royal Statistical Society*, December, 1890.

WAGNER, ADOLF, Allgemeine Volkswirtschaftslehre. Erster Theil, Grundlegung. Leipzig, 1894. 2te Ausgabe, 3tes Kapitel, pp. 223–251. This is a reference for specialists rather than the general reader. Wagner is noteworthy on account of his treatment of the legal basis and limitations of competition.

WALLACE, ALFRED RUSSEL, Studies Scientific and Social. 2 vols. New York, 1900. Vol. I, Chs. XIV to XVII inclusive, dealing with the Theory of Evolution, and Ch. XXIII, Human Selection. Vol. II, Ch. XXVIII, True Individualism the Essential Preliminary of a Real Social Advance.
Darwinism. London and New York, 1889.

WILLOUGHBY, W. W., Social Justice. New York, 1900. Ch. IX, The Ethics of the Competitive Process.

CHAPTER II

It is proposed, in this chapter, to treat somewhat more in detail a few points which are discussed only in a very cursory way in the preceding. A general view of competition has been presented, and an effort has been made to show that we have, in the stimulus and selection which competition affords, both a permanent and a beneficial economic and social force. While the present work aims to be suggestive rather than exhaustive, it is felt, nevertheless, that at least a few discriminations must be made, and a few features of competition further elucidated, in order that misunderstanding may be avoided and thought directed along right lines.[1]

It is obvious that the word "competition" is employed in a very wide sense so as to cover a multiplicity of activities, having in them little in common, except rivalry of one sort and another. The "Century Dictionary," it will be recalled, de-

---

[1] The author trusts that he may, without impropriety, repeat the statement that he hopes, in a later work in the Citizen's Library, to give a fuller treatment of competition under the title "Custom and Competition."

fines competition as "the act of seeking or endeavoring to gain what another is endeavoring to gain at the same time; common contest, or striving for the same object; strife for superiority; rivalry." We have rivalry in many different fields, as among plants and animals; we have among men contests of physical strength, and also emulation in artistic and intellectual pursuits; we have military and commercial rivalry among groups and societies; it will conduce to clear thinking if we consider some distinctions which should be made in the uses of terms.

Let us take up, first of all, the term "rivalry." We may distinguish between three main forms of rivalry.[1] The first main form of rivalry is struggle for existence. This is biological rivalry, and to be successful involves reproduction. "The essentials of biological rivalry are survival with subsequent production of offspring by and with physical heredity."[2] Biologically, then, a being might die of old age and yet not survive, in case this being has no offspring. The second form of rivalry is personal rivalry or emulation. It is the contest among individuals for personal advantage of some kind. Individuals contend with one another for the sake of economic gain, or it may be even for victory in some game of skill. It always involves the element

[1] The general classification found in the articles "Rivalry" and "Struggle for Existence" in the "Dictionary of Philosophy," edited by Professor J. Mark Baldwin, is followed at this point.

[2] Quoted from article "Rivalry" in the "Dictionary of Philosophy."

of consciousness, and is, therefore, psychological, and never simply biological, in the narrow sense of the term. In the third place, rivalry may be commercial and industrial, and becomes economic competition, which includes a large part of personal rivalry.

The struggle for existence is a struggle to maintain life and to leave offspring. This also takes three forms, following the classification of Professor Baldwin. There is first a struggle for food among animals when there is a deficiency on account of overpopulation. There is, in the second place, a struggle of animals with one another. This is not merely a struggle of individuals as individuals, but likewise a struggle of group with group. Even among the lower animals this is the case, as has already been pointed out in the preceding chapter. Among men this form of struggle becomes increasingly a struggle of group with group, and nation with nation. The third form of struggle is struggle with the obstacles which are imposed by the physical environment of animals, as heat, cold, etc. Adjustment is the process by which living beings succeed in meeting the conditions of inorganic environment. As a result of this struggle for existence, we have survival of those who are called the fittest; fittest, that is to say, with reference to conditions of time and place. It is to be noticed that biologists are laying increasing emphasis upon the second and third forms of struggle for existence, and not upon simple contests of one individual with another of like species, in order to secure food supply. This is especially significant when we come to the struggle among men, which is less and less a struggle for mere subsistence. It is true that there are very large numbers, and in older countries, even great classes, of men, who are struggling simply for the necessaries of life, but it is also true that this struggle is gradually receding into the background, inasmuch as it involves in civilized society a decreasing proportion of the population. Famine was once common in all countries, but has now practically disappeared in those economically most advanced. There are vast areas in the United States in which the problem of subsistence has been so far solved that the conscious struggle among men is almost altogether for something decidedly above subsistence.

The word "competition" is loosely used to cover all the meanings of rivalry and struggle for existence which have been mentioned; but in economic discussions it is limited to struggles for economic advantage, and perhaps generally it would be well to confine the word "competition" so far as possible to the realm of economics. When, however, we come to competition with an economic import we also have a great variety of meanings. Economic competition is not any struggle of conflicting interests, inasmuch as it would then include even criminal contests for advantage. This is a point, too, which has already been mentioned, but it needs to be emphasized, inasmuch as so many in the discussions of competition overlook the fact of its limitations by custom and law. Competition in the large economic sense may be formally defined as *the struggle of conflicting economic interests on the basis of the existing legal and social order for the sake of economic advantage of one sort or another.* Competition, then, undergoes a process of evolution and is capable of unlimited regulation, provided the element of rivalry is not removed. Modern competition rests upon a basis of property both public and private, and of contract, and certain laws and customs which regulate personal conditions, giving us servitude or freedom in their various forms. Property and contract themselves are regulated, and change with economic development. Competition, then, takes for granted the fundamental institutions of economic society, and these qualify and limit the struggle for existence.

Competition in a narrower sense is differentiated from bargaining. In this narrow sense competition consists of the rival efforts of those who desire precisely the same thing. It is a competition of carpenter with carpenter, of blacksmith with blacksmith, and, on the other hand, of employer with employer to secure the services of labor. As a result of the competition of workingman with workingman who offer the same kind of services, and of employer with employer who desire this kind of services, we have the conditions determined for the bargain which takes place between the two sides. It is the bargaining which directly determines the distribution of wealth, giving us wages, profits, rents, etc. Strikes are concerned with bargaining rather than with competition in this narrow sense. A good deal of the economic trouble of our time comes from the fact that employer does not compete with employer, and employee with employee, and thereby fix the terms of the bargain made between them; but that combination faces combination, and with the partial failure of competition to establish the bargain which results in wages, profits, etc., no adequate substitute has been found.

We have a great many different forms of competition besides those mentioned. We have what is called personal competition, which has in view competition largely as a principle of selection of men for posts in economic society, and is a principle of organization.[1]

A distinction is also frequently made between commercial competition and industrial competition. Commercial competition fixes prices on the market for the time being, and raises and lowers prices in an effort to bring about an equilibrium between supply and demand. Industrial competition is competition of investors, and of classes of manual and intellectual workers, of such a nature as to

[1] *Vide* " Personal Competition, its Place in the Social Order and Effect upon Individuals; with some considerations on Success," by Charles H. Cooley, Ph. D., American Economic Association, " Economic Studies," Vol. IV, No. 2.

equalize advantages of various pursuits and occupations. Competition of shoe manufacturer with shoe manufacturer is commercial competition; the shifting of capital from a less to a more profitable investment, and the shifting of a mechanic from an occupation which pays low wages to one which pays relatively high wages, gives industrial competition.[1]

It would take us too far from our present purpose to enter into a discussion of the various kinds of competition which could be mentioned; but one further distinction is especially important in the treatment of competition and monoply, and that is the distinction between competition and industrial war. This is a distinction which popular language makes, but which has not been often adequately elaborated by economic writers. Competition is a permanent, steady pressure, whereas industrial war among rivals implies destructive attacks, which aim at a cessation of hostilities in agreement or combination. The rivalry of one grocer with another gives us an illustration of normal competition, whereas the rivalry of two competing gas companies in one city furnishes us with an illustration of industrial war. The first pressure is constant and brings benefit to consumers; whereas the sort of struggle in which the gas companies engage frequently reduces prices far below cost and de-

---

[1] *Vide* Hadley's "Economics," Ch. III, § 100; also, Cairnes' "Some Leading Principles of Political Economy," Pt. I, Ch. III, especially § 5.

stroys values, the struggle keeping up until one party or the other is defeated, or until they can decide upon terms of cessation of hostilities, resulting in some kind of agreement or even consolidation. The adherents of the competitive order of society believe in the possibilities of that normal competition which exerts a regular pressure, and serves as a stimulus in the efforts of rivals to serve the public; whereas the socialists have generally believed that all competition must eventually become industrial war, which will prove the death of competition itself.

This naturally leads us to a discrimination between one of the aspects of economic competition and the biological struggle for life. The struggle for life is frequently a direct and immediate struggle, as where two dogs fight for the same bone. Competition is, in the main, an indirect process of securing results. We do not immediately and directly seek our food and clothing, but perform social services and receive a reward which we exchange for food and clothing. We render services to society, and society rewards us in what we receive in economic commodities and services. Where competition is at its best, the more we give the larger our reward. It is in this way that competition can be spoken of as "a game of give and not a game of get." [1]

As competition becomes in modern times, in the

[1] Quoted from an address by Professor J. B. Clark, before the New York State Conference of Religion, November 20, 1902.

most advanced countries, increasingly a struggle for something beyond subsistence, namely, a struggle for conventional necessaries, comforts, and luxuries and honors, can it be said that it results in selection? It has the beneficent effect of stimulation, but does it result in a selection which affects the race? Is it correct to say, as in the preceding chapter, that the reform of the civil service issues in the survival of men with qualities superior to those who survive under the spoils system? Directly and immediately we do not have in this case survival in the true biological sense. We have survival of certain traits which conduce to success, but indirectly competition must have an influence upon biological survival. Those who have the traits which are fittest for the existing environment are those who will advance most rapidly, and who will be in a position to marry at a comparatively early age, and who will also be favored in the selection of marriage.

It becomes plain from what has already been said that the competitive system does not mean of necessity a never ceasing scramble and a perpetual pushing for advantage. Within the competitive system there are protected positions which should be the reward of merit. This may be illustrated by the case of professors and judges. Excellence should be the test of appointment or election, but the position once secured it should not be continually called in question. The same holds with regard to many positions in private employment.

We have all sorts of boards and agencies of social control to encourage excellence within the competitive system. It is surprising, also, in view of much that is said about competition, to observe the general acquiescence in the rewards of competition when these are assigned on the basis of excellence. Complaint arises when something which is outside of and apart from the ability to serve society determines the selection. When in the private corporation favoritism prevails, and when in public life "pulls" determine appointments, we have disastrous consequences and pronounced dissatisfaction.

Property also protects men from the fiercest attacks of competition. The endeavor to secure a relatively protected position stimulates the efforts of men and leads to the accumulation of property. This is socially beneficial, and one of the most important lines of true social reform which can be suggested is the encouragement of accumulation of property through saving and frugal habits generally. It should be one of the special functions of government to afford opportunities for saving to those who are economically the weaker elements in the community, and to protect savings so as to have the widest possible diffusion of property. The arguments for postal savings-banks are conclusive, and have never been answered.

We must not go to the extreme position taken by some adherents of competition. Competition as it exists at present has its very grave evils, and a competitive system must always have its dark side. The position which a rational adherent of the competitive order takes is that to an ever increasing extent the evils of competition will be cured by the processes of social evolution, including individual and social self-conscious effort, and that, on the other hand, the evils which must remain are less than those of any other economic system, such as socialism.

Professor Baldwin shows in a most interesting manner, in his "Social and Ethical Interpretations," that the very processes of competition psychologically lead to the cultivation of altruism as well as egoism. Competition is a social process, and in it we must think of other selves as well as our own selves. We do necessarily picture situations to ourselves in which others are involved as well as ourselves, and we are forced to reflect upon the welfare of these others.

While adhering to competition we attempt to remove the worst abuses which now exist, such as those of the sweating system, the employment of young children, insanitary conditions in home and workshop, needless accidents to employees, particularly those of railways and great industrial establishments, and the adulteration of food products. Along all these lines we are making progress which can and should be greatly accelerated. There must necessarily remain economic evils which must be borne, and we have the opportunity for the cultivation of fortitude on the one hand and sympathy on the other. The need of the ethical teacher and the preacher will never cease.

Another line of importance is suggested by the observation that competition has done its work when old age comes on, and that every provision for honorable old age is desirable, which first is practicable, and which secondly does not discourage proper effort on the part of those who have not as yet reached old age. This suggests a large extension of insurance, and in time old-age pensions under suitable regulations.

In conclusion, it must be admitted that there remains what has been termed the human rubbish-heap of the competitive system. There are those who are not able to live in its strenuous atmosphere. The sad fact, however, is not that of competition, but the existence of these feeble persons. The sadness consists in the hard facts of life of which competition takes cognizance. If the weakest are favored and their reproduction encouraged, we must have social degeneration. The recognition of these hard facts, with suitable action taken with reference to them, reduces the amount of human pain for the present and the future by public and private charity. The socially rejected must be cared for and given as happy an existence as possible, provided only that we do not encourage the increase of those who belong to this sad human rubbish-heap.[1]

[1] This chapter is so closely related to the preceding one that no separate bibliography is required.

CHAPTER III

THE writer has taken the position in his treatment of competition that the altruism which has been developed in competitive society, and which has manifested itself in an infinite variety of methods for the alleviation of human suffering, prolongation of life, and the amelioration of man's social and physical environment, has been co-existent with the increasing strength and efficiency of men in modern civilized society. There are many who have taken a different position. Professor Alfred Marshall, the economist, has very grave apprehensions concerning the survival of the weak and feeble, who owe their survival to modern humanitarianism, modern medicine, and improvements in sanitation; while Mr. Alfred Russel Wallace, the great naturalist and co-worker with Darwin, tells us that on account of these modern improvements Darwin took a gloomy view of the future. But the present writer does not believe that these apprehensions are warranted by the facts in the case. Unfortunately, however, strange as it may seem, there never has been any serious investigation either by sociologists or biologists of the relative strength and vigor of man in the various stages of his evolution from savagery to the highest forms of civilization. There has been a great deal of talk on this subject, but no strictly scientific work. That there should be so much talk on the subject without any scientific basis, at first seemed to the writer so incredible that he felt obliged to ask his biological and sociological friends if they knew of any investigation into the facts which would warrant the frequent assertion of a dangerous decline in man's physical vigor. The same negative answer has been returned in every case.

The reasons for the view of a possible decline in vigor, due to modern improvements resting upon a combination of philanthropy and science, are obvious enough. The reasoning runs about as follows: Philanthropy and science keep alive men who would otherwise perish. These men reproduce their kind, and the result is an enfeebled progeny. Reproduction goes on, and as heredity determines chiefly the characteristics of those who live, we have a feebler parentage leading to a feebler race of men.

While assertions of this kind are frequently made, they produce comparatively little visible effect upon the growth of altruism and science. Even the most cold-blooded scientific men continue their researches, and aim both by preventive and curative methods to keep alive as many as possible, and to prolong the life of each individual to the utmost limit. The fund of altruistic sentiment continues to grow in the meantime. It would seem as if there were a very deep instinctive feeling that such good things as philanthropy and progress in knowledge could not, all appearances to the contrary notwithstanding, prove evil. The implications of the position that modern progress is leading to increasing survival of the unfit are truly startling. The great advances in medicine are in the region of preventive medicine, as it is called, which aims by general sanitary measures and correct mode of life to prevent disease, or at any rate to reduce it to its lowest terms. But if this is leading to an increasing number of an increasingly feeble population, should it not be checked? Man's increased power in the production of wealth means that it is easier than heretofore to furnish to all the necessities and even the comforts of life. The struggle for bare existence declines. If the view to which reference has been made is sound, should not efforts be put forth to hold back the wheels of industrial progress? May there not have been, then, a higher wisdom than has ever been supposed in the efforts of riotous workingmen in England, early in the last century, to smash machines? And what shall we say about the efforts in India to accumulate a famine fund, and extend and improve the means of communication so as to be able to fight famine successfully there as it has been fought successfully in Europe and America? Why not let the famine continue for the sake of race improvement?

We do continue our efforts, science advances, and philanthropy marches triumphantly forward. Nevertheless, here and there we do find a certain scepticism, and possibly in places a partial paralysis of efforts.

While we have not had the needed scientific investigation of the strength and vigor of man in the various stages of his evolution, an analysis of the forces at work certainly gives strong ground for the belief which the present writer has expressed that never before has there been such a high average of strength and vigor, and that never before has there been such promise of increasing strength and vigor for the future. It is true that some unfit persons are kept alive, and that some of these become parents. We must ask, however, first, is this number larger now than formerly? Is this number larger in the present stage of civilization than in the lower stages? Furthermore, in the second place, we must ask whether any forces have come into operation to offset, or more than offset, the fact that some now are kept alive who in an earlier civilization would have perished.

Taking up the first question, we may say that there is every indication that the number of the absolutely unfit has not increased, but, on the contrary, has in the most advanced countries tended to decline. The parasitical classes are the most unfit, and there is evidence that their number has been reduced. Statistics would seem clearly to indicate this in England, and probably in Germany. Where serious and long-continued efforts have been made in this country to reduce the number of these classes, moderate success appears to have been achieved. There have been earlier stages of civilization in which beggary was thought to be a virtue. It has even been asserted that in Cologne at one time one-fourth of the population consisted of paupers. Reports of travellers in countries of inferior civilization, such as India, lead us to think that the strength and vigor of this population is far below that of European countries. In any stage of civilization beyond the lowest, men and women are, as a rule, kept alive; and it is hopeless to expect that they will be allowed to perish because they are beings unfit for parentage. But it is in the higher stages of civilization that there is the most effort made to prevent parentage on their part.

Let us then take up the second line of inquiry, and ask what other forces are coming into operation which tend to secure race improvement. Race improvement is a result of selection on the one hand, and of environment on the other. When we speak of environment as the cause of improvement, we do not mean to imply the transmission of acquired qualities. It is very true, as Mr. Alfred Russel Wallace asserts, that you cannot secure race horses by cultivating speed in a miscellaneous assortment of horses, and giving them an environment suitable for racers. What a good environment does is to make the dray horses stronger dray horses, and to make them become the progenitors of a stronger race of dray horses. This is a truth upon which every man who is engaged in breeding acts daily. Our human problem is not to breed any one particular kind of men. We want all kinds of useful men, manual workers, skilled toilers, intellectual leaders. The improvement of environment gives us stronger and more vigorous men of all kinds. Among men and among animals we can, on every hand, see the results of an improved environment. It is shown in the statistics of the boys in schools, colleges, and universities, for the statistical examinations reveal a large and vigorous physique. It may be objected that there must have been a selective process among the parents, and this is a partial explanation; but more abundant food and more sanitary surroundings all have their effects. The more carefully one examines into the statistical data, the more strongly, it is believed, will one lay emphasis upon the importance of a good environment, giving us a larger number of strong and vigorous survivals.

There always will be some who are upon what we may call the ragged edge, those who just manage to live whether the conditions of life are more or less strenuous. This has always been, and must necessarily always be, the case. But what is the condition of those who are away from this ragged edge? The improvements of which we have spoken give them an improved physical outlook, and will lead to a better reproduction. If we think in the concrete and bring before our minds illustrations taken from our own experience, this will become clear. A gentleman, for years connected with one of the greatest hospitals in the country, tells the writer that long-continued illness in a family will at times reduce the whole family to the parasitical class. The family funds will become exhausted, the struggle to maintain a position among the self-supporting and self-respecting population will gradually be abandoned, and the whole family will sink to a lower plane. There begins a degradation which there is every reason to fear will continue into future generations.[1]

We have not only the physical heredity, but,

[1] The late Colonel Waring of New York City, who transformed the street-cleaning service of that city, in speaking about the prevention of deaths by sanitary measures, says that every one of these abnormal deaths means "forty times as many serious and corrupting illnesses." This is taken from Professor J. G. Brooks' recent work, "Social Unrest," p. 247. The statement by Colonel Waring could hardly be intended as a scientific estimate. Dr. Arthur Newsholme, in his "Vital Statistics," however, says that to the lives saved by improved sanitation we add "at least four times as many attacks of non-fatal diseases" (p. 151), and in speaking about the greater mortality of weakly children from infectious diseases in earlier times, he says: "We personally think that the weeding out of weakly lives, caused by the greater mortality among weakly children suffering from an infectious disease, is almost entirely counterbalanced by the greater number of children made weakly in former times by non-fatal diseases" (p. 316; this, like the preceding quotation, is from the third edition).

what has been so aptly termed by Professor J. Mark Baldwin, social heredity.[1] This social heredity means the general social environment, the thoughts, the habits, the ways of looking at things, the mental self-assertion on the part of the surrounding individuals. Now the social heredity of those who are born in a family which has fallen below the level of self-respect and self-maintenance is extremely bad. What does modern science and modern philanthropy do in cases of long-continued illness? One thing which is attempted is to provide for their proper treatment. Frequently they are obliged to leave hospitals before they are thoroughly cured. To provide for complete recovery, convalescents' homes are being established in connection with hospitals. Scientific charity attempts to place upon their feet those who have suffered from disease or from temporary misfortune.

But there are forces at work which must tend to improvements in the race due to selection. Never before since the days of Greece and Rome was more emphasis laid upon physical training, and never before was physical strength and prowess more highly esteemed. Even prize fighters are national heroes to whom the newspapers give up whole pages, where they give lines only to pure intellectual achievements. Athletic contests in our universities at times overshadow the intellectual work which we have heretofore supposed their

[1] In his "Social and Ethical Interpretations in Mental Development."

171

main purpose. No intellectual effort of a professor is heralded far and wide like the feats of a great athlete among the students. A true story brings out the attitude of the American boy. A lad in a preparatory school, visiting the University of Wisconsin, was quite excited when on the campus he met some one who was actually acquainted with the great football player, the punter, Pat O'Dea. The boy evidently felt himself honored to come as near the hero as this. Presently some one mentioned the president of the university, Dr. Adams, and he said, in a bewildered way, "Who is President Adams?"

Now along with this high esteem in which physical superiority is held goes an increasing freedom of women in their choice of husbands. More and more civilization allows women to choose among the various classes. More and more do modern conditions give them a wide range of choice, and this leads to a preference for men with superiority of some sort. Mr. Wallace, who has been so frequently quoted, looks to the increasing freedom of women as a means whereby the race will be improved. Female choice, he says, will result in a better natural selection. Mr. Wallace thinks that when women become economically more independent — and they actually are becoming more independent economically — a considerable number will feel not strongly inclined to marriage and will prefer to remain single rather than to take a husband who does not really satisfy them. On the other hand, with improvements which reduce accidents in industry, the number of men who will survive will be increased, and the women who do care to marry will have a larger range of choice. This cannot be elaborated further in this place.[1] It is interesting to notice that a woman who has written thoughtfully on "Women and Economics," Mrs. Charlotte Perkins Stetson,[2] expects that the greater economic freedom of women will result in improved selection of husbands.[3]

Let us next take up the degenerate classes, and ask whether any effort is being made to prevent their reproduction. Little has as yet been done, but in civilized society the subject has never before attracted so much attention, and never before probably has there as much been done as now to prevent their reproduction, while there is every reason to believe that a great deal more is going to be done in the future.

Criminals are confined for longer or shorter periods in jails or prisons, and they are, during this time, deprived of their opportunities for reproduction. The tendency of modern penology is to urge that criminals should be confined until thoroughly reformed, even if this results in life imprisonment. Those who are morally weak

[1] *Vide* "Studies, Scientific and Social," by Alfred Russel Wallace, Vol. I, p. 523, and especially Vol. II, pp. 507–508.

[2] Now Mrs. Gilman.

[3] "Women and Economics," by Charlotte Perkins Stetson, pp. 92, 110, 111, *et passim*.

should be placed where they cannot do any harm either directly themselves or indirectly through a degenerate posterity.

Paupers and feeble-minded are being placed in custodial institutions of one sort or another, and they are being denied, to an increasing extent, opportunies to become the parents of a vicious progeny. This means much.

Comparatively few people realize how strong is the quiet movement now going forward to regulate marriage, with a view to improve natural selection of those who are to continue the race. This movement can be traced back for at least forty years, and probably no one has been more worthily active in it than Mrs. Josephine Shaw Lowell, who, as member of various societies and organizations, has called attention to the conditions which have obtained in New York State. Investigations have been made from time to time during the past thirty years in New York, showing to how large an extent the most unfortunate classes in the community are the descendants of those who are physically, mentally, and morally absolutely unfit. One of Mrs. Lowell's pamphlets, entitled "One Means of Preventing Pauperism," shows the shocking condition of things which has existed in New York State from the motherhood of pauper and feeble-minded women. In this report she says, referring to the Tenth Annual Report of the New York State Board of Charities, "Even a casual perusal of this report will convince the reader that one of

the most important and most dangerous causes
of the increase of crime, pauperism, and insanity
is the unrestricted liberty allowed to vagrant and
degraded women."[1] She then goes on to give
the records of a few of the women found in
various poorhouses of the state. The Legislature
of New York State, in 1878, made provision for
the establishment of a home for feeble-minded
and idiotic pauper women. In 1880 this home
contained one hundred inmates. The result proves
to have been thoroughly satisfactory. It is said, in
the Report of the State Board of Charities for 1880,
that "the institution affords complete protection to
its inmates and thoroughly trains them to industrial
pursuits; and as the cost of maintenance and care
exceeds but little, if any, that of the poorhouses
and almshouses for the same class, it can no longer
be regarded as experimental. There are still considerable numbers of females of this class, in our
poorhouses and almshouses, who are without the
supervision and oversight adequate to their protection, and we believe it would be wise economy
for the state to extend its custodial accomodations
so as to include these."

The efforts begun in a feeble way have continued, and more and more has been accomplished
in New York State. The movement has also
spread to other states, where homes for the feeble-
minded have been established. As to the poor-

[1] "One Means of Preventing Pauperism," by Mrs. Josephine S.
Lowell, p. 3.

houses, we have reached a condition where at least the more intelligent portion of the community no longer consider it a joke when two pauper inmates are married. Doubtless we shall soon reach a time, as in older countries, when nothing of the sort will be tolerated.

But the regulation of marriage, which is proposed, and which is being pushed forward by physicians and thoughtful people, — by people who are the farthest removed from any possible designation as cranks, — looks beyond the prevention of the marriage of paupers and feeble-minded. A literature on this subject is growing up, as yet confined chiefly to medical journals and reports of medical associations. There lies before the writer the text of a law passed by Michigan, which prohibits the marriage of persons having certain maladies.[1] There also lie before him bills introduced in four legislatures, in 1901, to regulate marriage. These are the legislatures of Indiana, Ohio, Minnesota, and Wisconsin. The following is the full text of the Indiana bill of 1901, known as the Lindley Bill, from State Senator Thomas J. Lindley : —

" Be it resolved by the General Assembly of the State of Indiana, That it shall be the duty of the Governor of the State of Indiana immediately upon

---

[1] Law of 1899, Section 6, "No insane person, idiot, or person who has been afflicted with syphilis or gonorrhœa, and has not been cured of the same, shall be capable of contracting marriage."

the adjournment of the present session of the General Assembly to appoint five persons, eminent in their respective professions or spheres, two of whom shall be physicians, and one of whom shall be a man learned in the law, and two of whom shall be women who have been married and are mothers.

" It shall be the duty of the Commission to investigate and inquire into the laws pertaining to marriage and divorce, the physiological and hygienic effect of marriage under certain conditions and circumstances upon the offspring and society, and what are the rights, powers, and obligations of the State in the premises.

" It shall be the further duty of said Commission to make full report of their investigations, under the provisions of this resolution, and their conclusion reached, together with such recommendations relating thereto as to measures which may be adopted to remedy or mitigate evils now existing, which result in great domestic suffering and infelicity, and entail great expense upon society and the State; also to prepare and submit, as part of their report, a remedial bill for the consideration of the General Assembly of the State, which report and bill shall be submitted to the next regular session thereof, to be held in the city of Indianapolis in 1903.

" It shall be the duty of all public officers or other persons to assist said Commission in acquiring the information desired by answering questions and exhibiting records, and in all other proper ways."

Senator Lindley made the following statement concerning this bill: "For a long time my attention has been directed toward the necessity of having as much attention paid to the breeding of human beings as was devoted to the breeding of stock. On my farms I use science on animals that are not suitable to breed from. I reserve the very best. If I did not, my stock would run out and I would go to the poorhouse.

"There is complaint against the present divorce laws. Divorces are too common. Every one is allowed to mate and breed. Why not restrict those who are unsuitable to breed for the good of the human race?

"The Commission should provide for physical examination of all desiring to marry. This would include their racial tendencies, moral, mental, and physical condition, whether they are of sound mind, free from chronic deadly diseases, and not moral degenerates. If the several governments would devote a little attention to this subject for a few years, two generations would see a different people on this earth. It is a radical but sound idea." This bill failed of passage, as did the other bills referred to. In the present session (1903) Senator Lindley introduced another bill, from which the following is a quotation: —

"SECTION I. Be it enacted by the General Assembly of the State of Indiana, That it shall be unlawful for any clerk of the court, deputy clerk,

or any other officer who may hereafter be authorized to issue marriage licenses, after having received notice, to grant such licenses to persons,
either one of whom shall be at the time of making application therefor confined in any jail, prison,
or workhouse upon any criminal charge, or under
bonds therefor; or to any couple, either one of
whom shall be a pauper or public charge, the
woman being under fifty years of age; or to any
person afflicted or supposed to be afflicted with
epilepsy, tuberculosis, or syphilis, unless such person shall procure from a local health officer of the
State, county, municipality, or town in which such
applicant resides, a sworn statement in writing that
such applicant is not afflicted with such disease."

This bill, after passing the Senate, failed in the
House, as did the bill in 1901. The first bill,
however, is really preferable, in order that legislative action may be preceded by ample and scientific
inquiry. This movement is, as already intimated,
but in its infancy. But, with the kind of people
who are pushing it forward, there is every promise
that it is going to attain great prominence. The
results will be, in time, a considerable degree of
elimination of the most unfit for parentage.[1] This

[1] In this connection it should be observed that the last Congress
by an act approved March 3, 1903, has provided for the exclusion
from our immigrants of the most unfit classes. This act should be
viewed as simply one manifestation of a growing desire and de-
termination on the part of the people of the United States to raise
the quality of our population. The following is a quotation from the

itself, as an advance beyond what the world has
seen heretofore, means much. It is also entirely
in line with what is desired in accordance with Mr.
Wallace's statement: "What we want is not a
higher standard of perfection in the future, but a
higher average, and this can best be produced by
the elimination of the lowest of all, and the free
intermingling of the rest." [1]

Apart from legislative effort, private action must
be affected by enlightenment, and an improved
sentiment concerning marriage, with the result
that, voluntarily at least, more of the physically
unfit will refrain from marriage.

It is, perhaps, not quite true that, apart from
the really unfit in the community, we desire a free
act just mentioned: " All idiots, insane persons, epileptics, and persons who have been insane within five years previous; persons who
have had two or more attacks of insanity at any time previously;
paupers; persons likely to become a public charge; professional
beggars; persons afflicted with a loathsome or with a dangerous con-
tagious disease; persons who have been convicted of a felony, or
other crime or misdemeanor involving moral turpitude; polygamists,
anarchists, or persons who believe in or advocate the overthrow by
force or violence of the Government of the United States, or of all
government, or of all forms of law, or the assassination of public officials; prostitutes, and persons who procure or attempt to bring in
prostitutes or women for the purpose of prostitution; those who have
been, within one year from the date of the application for admission
to the United States, deported as being under offers, solicitations,
promises or agreements to perform labor or service of some kind
therein; and also any person whose ticket or passage is paid for
with the money of another, or who is assisted by others to come, unless it is affirmatively and satisfactorily shown that such person does
not belong to one of the foregoing excluded classes."

[1] "Studies, Social and Scientific," Vol. I, p. 525.

intermingling of all the rest of the population. We desire our racers, as well as our draught horses, but natural and sexual selection seem to be quite able to take care of this matter. We do have a great deal of selection going on. Like marry like, the old adage to the contrary notwithstanding, and we shall have intellectually and spiritually superior families in the future quite as much as in the past.

We have much to learn as to who are the fit physically and mentally, and as to the measures to secure the best reproduction. What is here stated must be regarded as only suggestions, which, it is hoped, will be followed up by others, and upon which the writer will be glad himself to do further work, if leisure therefor can be found. The writer can in this place only describe such thoughts and observations as have convinced him that never before has there been a higher degree of vigor in modern nations, and never before have more promising efforts been made to maintain, and even to increase, man's physical powers and economic efficiency.

LITERATURE

The literature of this subject is so vast, is found in so many books and magazines, is quite largely so difficult and technical, and is also, for the purposes of the present chapter, for the most part, so unsatisfactory, that the attempt to give references is at the outset discouraging. It would be possible to write an entire book upon the literature, but it is not easy to mention comparatively few works which will prove helpful to the ordinary reader. Nevertheless, several titles are given below. Should there be those desiring to carry the study farther, the publications mentioned will put them in the way of still further sources of information.

BILLINGS, J. S., The Diminishing Birth-rate in the United States. The Forum, June, 1893.

BROWNELL, J. L., The Significance of the Decreasing Birth Rate. Annals of the American Academy of Political and Social Science, July, 1894, Vol. V.

BRYCE, JAMES, Relations of the Advanced and Backward Races of Mankind. Romanes Lecture. Oxford, 1902.

DICTIONARY OF PHILOSOPHY. J. Mark Baldwin, editor. New York, 1903. Consult articles dealing with authors and topics mentioned in this chapter.

EDSON, CYRUS, American Life and Physical Deterioration. North American Review, October, 1893.

FETTER, FRANK A., Social Progress and Race Degeneration. The Forum, October, 1899.

GALTON, FRANCIS, Hereditary Genius. New York, 1871.

GIDDINGS, FRANKLIN H., Principles of Sociology. New York, 1896. Bk. III, The Historical Evolution of Society. Bk. IV, Social Process, Law and Cause.

JORDAN, DAVID STARR, The Blood of the Nation. Boston, 1902. Emphasizes (and perhaps too strongly) the influence of war in removing many of the stronger men and thus leading to race deterioration. The modern railway, at least in the United States, injures and destroys more men than modern war. Those who have access to the Army and Navy Journal will do well to read in this connection an article which appeared in the issue for July 21, 1900, entitled "The Hell of Railroading"— taken of

course from the familiar statement that "war is hell."
It is very well that Dr. Jordan has called attention to the
significance of war in race deterioration, but a full scientific account of the forces at work in determining the
character of the race must take note also of industrial
accidents which kill so many more men. Nor can it in a
scientific inquiry be assumed, without careful investigation, that the men who are destroyed by industry, especially the railways, are less valuable considered as fathers
than the men who are destroyed by war. These remarks
are pertinent as calling attention to the scientific aspects
of the case. Practical philanthropy will lead us to inquire whether or not in the case of war we may avoid
this loss, and whether or not in the case of industry we
can afford the expenditure which would prevent bodily
injuries and the loss of life; since by far the larger proportion of accidents to employees, especially to those of
railways, are preventable.

KUCZYNSKI, R. R., The Fecundity of the Native and Foreign-
born Population in Massachusetts. Quarterly Journal
of Economics, November, 1901, and February, 1902.
Vol. XVI.

NEWSHOLME, ARTHUR, The Elements of Vital Statistics.
3d ed., "almost entirely rewritten." London and New
York, 1899. In the discussion of Social Progress and
Race Improvement, Ch. XV on The Influence of Climate
and Social Conditions on Mortality, and Ch. XXVI on
The Decline in the English Death Rate and its Causes
are especially valuable. But the whole work may be
recommended since a knowledge of vital statistics, "the
science of numbers applied to the life history of communities and nations," will be an aid to the serious
student in avoiding many pitfalls in the discussion of this
complicated subject.

PACKARD, A. S., Lamarck, the Founder of Evolution. New
York, 1901. The last chapter is a statement of the principles of Neo-Lamarckism.

PEARSON, KARL, Chances of Death, and other Essays in Evolution. London and New York, 1897.

PEARSON, KARL, A Grammar of Science. 2d ed. London, 1900. Ch. IX, Life; Ch. X, Evolution (Variation and Selection); Ch. XI, Evolution (Reproduction and Inheritance).

RITCHIE, D. G., Darwin and Hegel. London and New York, 1893. Ch. I, note on Heredity as a Factor in Knowledge. Ch. II, Darwin and Hegel. As the title indicates, this is an examination of the scientific relation between the two great leaders of thought named, and also an inquiry into the biological controversy between the Lamarckian and Weismannite. Ritchie is critical and always thought-provoking.

Darwinism and Politics. 2d ed. London, 1891.

ROWNTREE, B. SEEBOHM, Poverty: a Study of Town Life. 3d ed. New York, 1902. Especially Ch. VII, The Relation of Poverty to the Study of Town Life.

WARD, LESTER F., Outlines of Sociology. New York, 1898. Ch. XI, Individual Telesis; Ch. XII, Collective Telesis.

Psychic Factors of Civilization. Ch. XXXVIII, Sociocracy, and Ch. XXXIV, Meliorism.

Pure Sociology. New York, 1903. It is difficult to make a selection of chapters, but perhaps Ch. XI, Social Dynamics; Ch. XIX, Conquests of Nature; and Ch. XX, Socialization of Achievement, may be specially mentioned.

WEISMANN, AUGUST, Essays in Heredity. 2 vols. Oxford, 1891.

WELLS, H. G., Mankind in the Making. Cosmopolitan Magazine, November, 1902.

Human Evolution an Artificial Process. Fortnightly Review, Vol. LX.

APPENDIX A

INSTITUTIONS FOR THE FEEBLE-MINDED IN THE UNITED STATES

For the following brief account of the establishment of institutions for feeble-minded in this country, the present writer is indebted to Dr. A. W. Wilmarth, Superintendent of the Wisconsin Home for Feeble-minded at Chippewa Falls.

"In Massachusetts, January 22, 1846, a committee of the House of Representatives were ordered to consider the expediency of appointing commissioners to inquire into the condition of idiots in the commonwealth," to ascertain their number, and whether anything could be done for their relief. On the report of this commission, the legislature appropriated $2500 for an experimental school.

"In New York, in the same year, a bill was introduced into the Senate, but failed in the Assembly. This was repeated in 1849, 1850, 1851, when the first legislation was effected by the passage of an act entitled 'An Act to establish an Asylum for Idiots and making an appropriation therefor.'

"In 1848 a private school was opened at Barre, Mass., which is still in successful operation.

"The first legislation in Pennsylvania was that which established, on April 7, 1853, the Pennsylvania Training School at Germantown.

"April 17, 1857, the Ohio legislature passed a bill creating the Ohio Institution for Feeble-minded.

"The Board of Commissioners, whose investigation led to the establishment of the Connecticut School for Feeble-minded was appointed in 1855.

"Kentucky granted the charter for the Kentucky Institution February 11, 1860.

"Illinois started an experimental school for the teaching of these children as an adjunct of the Deaf Mute Institution at Jacksonville, shortly after Kentucky had taken action.

"Institutions were organized in Iowa in 1876, in Minnesota in 1879, in Indiana in the same year.

"The Kansas Institution was established in 1881, that of California in 1883, and that of Nebraska in 1887.

"Maryland purchased a site for its institution in 1888. New Jersey started with two institutions about the same time.

"Washington opened separate accommodations for the feeble-minded in 1891.

"Michigan began operations in 1895.

"The legislature of Wisconsin made an appropriation for the erection of buildings in that state in 1895, though the buildings were not occupied until early in 1897.

"Pennsylvania opened a second institution in the western part of the state the same year. North Dakota is opening an institution at Grafton. In Colorado, New Hampshire, and Maine, active work is being done towards organizing this work in those states."

In another letter Dr. Wilmarth calls attention, in the following language, to another important consideration : —

"There is one passage in your article that attracted my attention especially : ' But with all its mildness, civilization lessens unfit reproduction, and on the whole does so to an ever increasing extent,' etc. I think that is liable to be more true in the future than it has been in the past. It has, indeed, put the feeble-minded in asylums, where it has educated some of them to an extent that they are able to go out, earn some kind of a living, naturally marry some one of about their own grade of intelligence, and, sad to say, in some cases produce a large family of defectives. It places the insane in hospitals, allows them to return to their families even before recovering, and invariably so as soon as such symptoms have passed as would make them a menace to the community.

"I see in the Report of the Conference of Charities in Topeka, that Hon. J. D. Alexander states : ' We have in the Institution for the Feeble-minded (in Ohio) eleven imbeciles that are the children of a person taken into that institution thirty years ago, and then allowed to go out to bring back a brood of imbeciles.' The authorities in this state have wisely taken the ground that imbecile girls committed to our care should stay with us until the age of forty-five, unless we are assured that they are going into perfectly safe care. When we can check the flood of degeneracy from this source, we shall not only have the advance which you describe, but we shall check in large measure the current flowing in the opposite direction. I think the state should pass laws sufficiently strong to curb indiscriminate marriage, and yet not so radical as to make them inoperative. I know of no better law yet framed than that in Connecticut, which punishes any one marrying an insane, feeble-minded, or epileptic person, and imposes a penalty on any one who aids or abets such a marriage."

APPENDIX B

CONNECTICUT LAW REGULATING MARRIAGE[1]

§ 1354. *Marriage of Epileptics and Imbeciles.* — Every man and woman, either of whom is epileptic, imbecile, or feeble-minded, who shall intermarry, or live together as husband and wife, when the woman is under forty-five years of age, shall be imprisoned not more than three years. But nothing herein contained shall be construed as affecting the mutual relations of any man and woman lawfully married on or before the thirty-first of July, 1895. — 1895, Chs. 325, 350.

§ 1355. *Procuring or aiding such Marriage.* — Every person who shall advise, aid, abet, cause, or assist in procuring the marriage of the persons described in § 1354, knowing them or either of them to be epileptic, imbecile, or feeble-minded, shall be fined not more than one thousand dollars, or imprisoned not more than five years, or both. — 1895, Ch. 325.

§ 1356. *Penalty for Carnal Knowledge in Certain Cases.* — Every man who shall carnally know any female under the age of forty-five years who is epileptic, imbecile, feeble-minded,

[1] From Revised Statutes of Connecticut, 1902.

or a pauper, shall be imprisoned not more than three years. Every man, who is epileptic, who shall carnally know any female under the age of forty-five years, and every female under the age of forty-five years who shall consent to be carnally known by any man who is epileptic, imbecile, or feeble-minded, shall be imprisoned not more than three years. — 1895, Ch. 325.

§ 1357. *Joining Persons in Marriage without Authority.* — Whoever undertakes to join persons in marriage, knowing that he is not authorized so to do, shall be fined not more than five hundred dollars, or imprisoned not more than one year, or both. — 1865, Rev. 1888, § 1561.

CHAPTER IV

MONOPOLIES AND TRUSTS

I. *General Statement of the Problem*

First of all, it is essential that we should have a clear idea of monopoly as a starting-point. To use the language of the philosopher Locke, the word "monopoly" is a sign standing for an idea. What is that idea? Unless we know exactly what it is that we are talking about when we are discussing monopoly our own thought will be confused, and the confusion will be multiplied many fold when the discussion becomes general. There can be no doubt that in economic literature, as well as in the periodical press, this one word-sign, monopoly, has been made to stand for many different and more or less antagonistic ideas, and as a consequence the controversies in which we have been engaged concerning monopoly have produced comparatively little action and even less light. Undoubtedly the economists are quite largely responsible for the confusion of thought which has been introduced into the discussion of monopoly, for, extending the term to cover related but quite different economic concepts, they have departed

from the best usage of the English language.
The courts in their decisions have not gotten so
far away from the correct use of language, but
their decisions also show confusion of thought,
due to the fact that they have frequently attempted
to introduce ideas appropriate to the seventeenth
century into recent decisions without that modification which the mighty industrial evolution of
three centuries has necessitated.

To what do we oppose most sharply the word
" monopoly " in our thought ? The answer at once
given is competition. Monopoly is the opposite
of competition. Competition means, among other
things, rivalry in the offer of services or commodities. When each one of two or more persons
seeks to induce us to purchase of him, and not of
others, services or commodities which he has for
sale, we have a condition of competition. Whenever, on the contrary, we have only one seller, we
have a condition of monopoly ; and we have only
one seller when all those who have services or
commodities of a particular kind for sale have so
bound themselves together that they act as one
man. What has been said with respect to sales
would also hold true with respect to purchases.
It is unity in some one kind of business which
gives us monopoly. The following is then offered
as a definition of monopoly which accords with
good English usage : *Monopoly means that substantial unity of action on the part of one or more
persons engaged in some kind of business which*

gives exclusive control more particularly, although not solely, with respect to price.

It is not now possible to discuss this definition exhaustively.[1] One or two things, however, must be said. What is essential is control of price. The other things which monopoly carries with it flow from such control and are not secure without it. In the second place, the fact must be emphasized that absolute unity of action is not requisite. The essence of monopoly is *substantial and controlling* unity of action, and this is given when a combination of men acting together as a unit have a dominating position over the sale of some one kind of commodity or service. Mr. Havemeyer, president of the American Sugar Refining Company, at one time said that a man producing eighty per cent of the product had such a position. The percentage, however, is a variable one.

The definition of monopoly which is here given brings before us its social significance in several most important particulars. As it is the opposite of competition, so the protection which competition gives to society is removed by monopoly. The theory of competition is that we are protected against unreasonable demands by the rivalry existing among competitors. The farmer who is tempted to ask an exorbitant price for his potatoes is held in check by his neighbors who have potatoes which they likewise desire to sell. The retail merchant

[1] The entire subject is discussed at far greater length in the author's work, " Monopolies and Trusts."

who places an excessive valuation upon his services finds that his rivals, more moderate in their demands, take away his customers from him. This is all simple enough, but it has a profound meaning which has made a deep impress upon English common law. Competition has been regarded for ages as a corner-stone of our industrial order, while monopoly has been held to be a menace to that order. The decisions of courts, both in our own country and England, proceed upon the hypothesis that competition is the palladium of our industrial liberties. It is true that competition is a corner-stone of our present social order. If competition is removed, something else must be put in place of it. It is because this truth has been so clearly grasped by socialism, and because socialism does propose to put something else in the place of competition, that the logical position of socialism has proved so strong. It is essential that we should clearly grasp the fact that we must have competition or something else in the place of it. If this is so, the popular apprehension in regard to the growth of monopoly does not exaggerate its significance, however confused and perplexed public opinion may be in other particulars. The next question which suggests itself naturally is this : To what extent does monopoly actually prevail? Has competition been replaced to such an extent that the competitive order has been seriously disturbed? If we cannot give a precise and definite answer to the first question, there can be no doubt that the second question calls for a decided affirmation in reply. Appeal may be made to the familiar experience of all. We continually run up against monopoly in one way or another, and we feel that we lack the protection which full and free competition would afford. It may be that we have to do practically with one employer wherever we seek work. It may be that in the sale of our product we encounter purchasers so allied that they act as one man. It may be that in our own purchases of services we feel ourselves powerless because we are pitted against vast combinations of interests which are completely unified. Probably there will be few adult readers of these words who have not felt themselves hurt and aggrieved by what they deemed the conscienceless action of monopoly. We may, however, approach the subject more analytically and scientifically if we examine into the classification and causes of monopoly. This is essential if we are to think clearly on the subject of monopolies and trusts. One main reason why we have made so little practical and so comparatively little scientific progress in the treatment of this subject is attributable to the failure to analyze and classify very complex forces and phenomena, and the result has been that we have been dealing with things essentially different as if they were all one in kind.

There are many different points of view from which we may regard monopolies, and consequently many different classifications. The following classification, based on causes of monopoly, is one which has proved especially helpful to the author in his own thought : —

A. SOCIAL MONOPOLIES.
    I. General Welfare Monopolies.
        1. Patents.
        2. Copyrights.
        3. Public Consumption Monopolies.
        4. Trade-marks.
        5. Fiscal Monopolies.
    II. Special Privilege Monopolies.
        1. Those based on Public Favoritism.
        2. Those based on Private Favoritism.

B. NATURAL MONOPOLIES.
    I. Those arising from a Limited Supply of Raw Material.
    II. Those arising from Properties Inherent in the Business.
    III. Those arising from Secrecy.

This classification of monopolies brings before us, by the analysis which it presents, the wide sweep of monopoly in modern industrial society. The simple enumeration itself does that, even without explanation of the various classes and subclasses. A few words, however, about some of these classes are essential.

A Social Monopoly is a monopoly which arises out of social arrangements and is an expression of the will of society as a whole, through government, or

194

of a section of society strong enough to impose its will on society. A Natural Monopoly, on the other hand, is a monopoly which rests back on natural arrangements as distinguished from social arrangements.

The term "natural" here is used in its well-understood and customary sense, to indicate something external to man's mind. A natural monopoly is one which, so far from giving expression to the will of society, grows up apart from man's will and desire, as expressed socially, and frequently in direct opposition to his will and desire thus expressed.

Public consumption monopolies are monopolies designed to regulate consumption beneficially, either to promote some desirable consumption, or to restrict and confine within limits deleterious and injurious consumption. The alcohol monopoly of Switzerland, the Japanese opium monopoly in Formosa, and the South Carolina dispensary system afford illustrations. Fiscal monopolies are monopolies which are created primarily in the interest of the public treasury. The tobacco monopoly of France affords the best illustration. Monopolies based on public favoritism are monopolies which are due primarily to the action of public authority exerted in the interest of favorites. The old Tudor monopolies, against which protest was made so frequently in our early constitutions, afford abundant illustrations. Hume gives a vivid description of them in the reign of Elizabeth, in his "History of England." Private favoritism

monopolies are businesses not naturally monopolistic, which have become monopolies by virtue of
an alliance with another monopoly, especially a
natural monopoly, whereby they partake of the
properties of the latter. Here special reference is
made to the favoritism of railways, which has been
so potent a cause of monopoly in the United
States. This is well known, probably, to most
people, and so far as the sceptical are concerned,
it is in this place sufficient simply to refer to the
reports of the Interstate Commerce Commission.
The question may arise, however, why monopolies
resting back on private favoritism are called social
monopolies. It is true that they do not express
the will of society as a whole; on the other hand,
they do give expression to the will of a social class
strong enough to make its purposes prevail in
society, and they are furthermore social because
society is responsible for their existence, inasmuch
as it is the function of society to prevent their
existence.

Those monopolies arising from properties inher-
ent in the business are those ordinarily designated
as natural monopolies, although here they are presented simply as one subclass under the general
term. They are railways, telephones, gas-works,
etc. We have two other classes of natural monopolies. The first of these classes consists of monopolies based upon a supply of raw material so limited
that the sources of supply have been brought under
unified control. Either one man has secured the

sources of supply, or a combination of men who act together with substantial unity. Anthracite coal affords a familiar illustration. As time goes on it is not unlikely that other sources of supply will be monopolized. It is a question on the one hand of limitation of sources and the wealth which can be brought under unified control. The more limited the supply and the higher the degree of concentrated ownership of wealth, the easier will be the formation of this kind of monopoly. Secrecy is one cause of monopoly, and to this increasing importance is apparently attached by manufacturers. It is placed under the head Natural Monopolies, because it is due to the private action of individuals and is not the expression of a conscious purpose of society.

It is hardly too much to say that the value of all monopolized businesses in the United States more probably exceeds a sixth of the entire valuation of property in the United States than falls short of this proportion.

If we have now a clear idea of what monopoly means, and of the extent to which it prevails, the next question which naturally suggests itself is this: What precisely is the power of monopoly? The specific power of monopoly is that which arises from unified action on the part of monopolists. It is especially, although not exclusively, a power over price, and has been felicitously described by a German economist as unified tactics with respect to price. We should, however, in connection with our inquiries into the power of monopoly, give attention to the other things than the power to raise price which monopoly carries with it. This is especially important, inasmuch as almost exclusive attention has been directed to the power of monopoly to raise price. The one who is a monopolist, as he has exclusive control over his products, can, for that very reason, withhold supplies or services or furnish them irregularly. If we examine into the power of railways to help forward their favorites and to crush those whom they will, we must not think by any means merely of freight rates. If rates are uniform, while of two competitors one always receives cars when he wants them and the other has difficulty in securing cars for shipment, or if the freight of the one is forwarded promptly while the freight of the other is frequently sidetracked, this alone will sometimes be sufficient to build up the one and to ruin the other. We must also direct our attention to everything connected with railway terminals, for in special advantages connected with these lies a large monopoly power, and in some cases these are alone a sufficient force to produce monopoly.[1] An illustration is afforded by the transfer of passengers and baggage between railway stations in many American cities.

But in addition to the power to raise price, we must also take into account the power to lower

[1] In the case of the United States against the " Beef Trust," the government makes a special point of advantages of this kind as well as special freight rates.

price, which is often equally effective. If, after I get in my supplies, you, my rival, order yours and secure transportation at lower rates, you have an advantage over me which may prove sufficient to enable you to drive me from business. How easy it is for those in a secret combination to aid one another with advance information concerning changes in monopolistic prices! and frequently it will make no difference whether prices are to be raised or lowered.[1]

It is true, however, that what we have to consider principally in the case of monopoly is the high profits which the monopolist can secure. It is this excess of price especially which is of vital significance in the distribution of wealth. It has long been said that the monopolist charges that price which enables him to secure the highest net returns. The monopolist having control over supply may in one way charge what price he pleases, as the courts so often state that he does. He must, however, charge a price which will enable him to dispose of his product. He does have control over supply, but he does not have control over consumption. If people refuse to buy his services or commodity, he has no sales and no profits. He

---

[1] The various monopolistic devices to bring other producers into harmonious action with monopolistic concerns are well called clubbing by Professor John B. Clark, in his "Control of Trusts" (*e.g.* p. 59). Mr. George L. Bolen, in his "Plain Facts as to the Trusts and the Tariff," gives description of different methods of wielding the "monopoly club." Consult the references under that term in the Index of his book.

must reduce prices until he has that combination of sales and profits on each sale which will give him the highest net returns.

This is all more or less familiar ground, but there is something that is still more fundamental, and that the author has endeavored to formulate in a new law of monopoly price, which is as follows : *Other things being equal, the greater the intensity of customary use, the higher the general average of economic well-being, and the more readily wealth is expended, the higher the monopoly charge which will yield the largest net returns.*[1]

The significance of the intensity of customary use is something which cannot now be discussed, but it is desired to direct attention particularly to the other features of this law of monopoly price. The higher the general average of well-being, other things being equal, the higher the price which people will pay for commodities or services rather than go without them. Consequently this furnishes the monopolist with an opportunity for greater gains than those which could be reaped in a country with a lower average of well-being. Similarly, the more readily people spend money, the higher will be the price which will yield the largest net returns, because the higher the price which people will pay for commodities or services rather than forego their enjoyment. We find these two conditions in high degree meeting together in the United States,

[1] This and other points are further elaborated in the author's " Monopolies and Trusts."

and this explains why it is that monopoly is among us so especially profitable. Probably there is no other country in the world in which monopoly, if let alone, yields such large returns as in our own country. Again, there is no other country among the great civilized nations of the world in which monopoly has been so let alone, so far as any real effective control is concerned, as it has been in the United States. We have, then, in the law of monopoly price a partial explanation of the vast concentration of wealth in the United States. We have abundant illustrations on every hand of the vast fortunes which monopolistic pursuits have yielded in our country, and we have an explanation of them which will, the writer believes, appeal to his readers and which, indeed, in his opinion, will grow upon them the more they think about it. We may take as an illustration street-car fares in our own country and in other countries. There is evidence going to show that the price for street-car service in our great American cities which yields the largest net returns to the street-car monopolist is five cents. Apart from all legislative control, it is not probable that in our great cities it is in the interest of the owners of street-car property to charge more than five cents. With our high average of well-being and our readiness in the expenditure of money, a five-cent fare reaches down into the masses of the people. Doubtless it is too high a fare for the lowest social strata, and yet it reaches so far down that probably the in-

crease in traffic from a lower fare would not offset the loss in profit on each passenger transported.
In a country like Germany, on the other hand, a
five-cent fare would probably be too high to yield
the largest net return to the monopolist, inasmuch
as, with the lower general average of economic
well-being and the greater frugality, a fare so high
would not reach down far enough into the masses
of the people to induce a sufficiently large traffic
to be most remunerative. The fare in Berlin for
one of their zones is 10 pfennige or 2.4 cents, and
the writer is strongly inclined to think that that is
the fare which yields the largest net returns. Our
telephone service affords another illustration. It
is safe to express the opinion that in a city like
Berlin the charges for telephone service which
large numbers pay in New York and Chicago
would so reduce the use of the telephone that it
would not be highly remunerative.

Our discussion of monopolies has brought before
us the evils of monopoly. It may be well to add,
in further elucidation of these evils, a quotation
from a leading British case known as the Case of
Monopolies. It is the case of Darcy *vs.* Allein of
1602. The court stated the evils of monopoly in
these words : —

"First. 'The price of the same commodity will be
raised, for he who has the sole selling of any commodity
may and will make the price as he pleases. . . . The second
incident to a monopoly is that after the monopoly is
granted the commodity is not so good and merchantable

as it was before ; for the patentee, having the sole trade, regards only his private benefit, and not the common-wealth. Third. It tends to the impoverishment of divers artificers and others, who, before, by the labor of their hands in their art or trade, have maintained them-selves and their families, who now will of necessity be constrained to live in idleness and beggary.' "

This exposition of evils has been very frequently indorsed by American courts, and one of these courts adds this comment upon the third ground mentioned : " The third objection, though fre-quently overlooked, is none the less important. A society in which a few men are the employers and the great body are merely employees or ser-vants, is not the most desirable in a republic ; and it should be as much the policy of the laws to multiply the numbers engaged in independent pur-suits or in the profits of production as to cheapen the price to the consumer. Such policy would tend to an equality of fortunes among its citizens, thought to be so desirable in a republic, and lessen the amount of pauperism and crime."

We have, then, on the one hand the oppression and tyranny which must flow from monopoly in a society composed of human beings, and on the other hand we have the inequalities in opportunity which discourage effort in two directions. Those who have these exclusive opportunities are not so alert and active as they would be otherwise, inas-much as they rely upon monopoly rather than upon excellence and energy in their economic

efforts, while those who find themselves so handi-
capped in the race for economic well-being are apt
to become listless and indifferent as the result of
discouragement. We are speaking now, not about
what happens in the early days of monopoly, but
what must happen in the long run as the result of
well-known principles of human nature. We have,
then, as a further outcome of the evils mentioned,
a degree of concentration of wealth which affords
to some opportunities for indulgence of every whim
and caprice, with wild extravagance as the result,
while others lack the opportunities for a full and
harmonious development of their faculties. Without entering into this farther at present, it may be
said that history furnishes abundant evidence of
the pernicious social effects of wanton luxury con-
fronted by poverty. Lecky's "History of European Morals" gives a conservative statement of
the ethical consequences of luxury. That great
thinker, Aristotle, whose wise words still have
deep meaning, may be consulted for a discussion
of the difficulties of uniting wide extremes in the
distribution of wealth with political democracy.
Our courts do not at all exaggerate the dangers of
monopoly, even if they do not always clearly see
the direction in which remedies must be sought.

This chapter is entitled "Monopolies and
Trusts," but thus far nothing has been said about
trusts. The reason why nothing has been said
about trusts is because, in the strict sense of the
word, there is no such thing as a trust problem.

Until we have this clearly in mind, we can make no progress in our discussion of monopolies and trusts. The trust in itself is no problem. But this must not be misunderstood. When men talk about trusts they are discussing real and vital problems, and analysis will show that, in so far as the discussion of the trust problem is an intelligent discussion, it resolves itself into three problems : first of all, and chiefly, a monopoly problem; secondly, a problem of concentration in production; and thirdly, a problem of wealth concentration, — quite a different thing from the problem of concentration of production. Concentration of production means large-scale production. It means the great factory and the mammoth department store. Concentration of production has its own problems, but these may coexist with the keenest competition, as they usually do in both the cases just mentioned. Large-scale production, when it comes about as the result of the free play of economic forces, is justified by its efficiency. When it is able to maintain itself in a fair field without favors it gives a large return for expenditures of capital power and human labor power. It adds thus to the provision for human comfort, and should be no more antagonized than machinery should be. The real problem is to utilize it fully while reducing to a minimum any evils incident to it. Many of the evils which large-scale production originally brought have already been mitigated by humane legislation which has regulated conditions of employment. Reference is made especially to what is popularly known as factory legislation, which prohibits the employment of young children, and regulates beneficially sanitary conditions surrounding wage-earners, and otherwise helps them to maintain wholesome conditions of life. Other evils which concentration of production has brought are those which investors have suffered on account of dishonest management of great enterprises, and for this relief must be sought in the improvement of our law governing private corporations. Something ,more will be said about this remedy presently.

II. *Analysis of the Steel Trust*

Let' us now consider these principles as applied to the greatest of all trusts, the United States Steel Corporation. Articles on this billion-dollar trust — or more accurately speaking, billion-and-a-half-dollar trust — have mostly regarded this new gigantic enterprise as a unit. It is a unit as a business undertaking, but on its economic side it is a unit which is made up of varied and complex parts and forces, and it cannot be understood as a manifestation of industrial evolution unless we analyze it.

It is an undoubted fact that in this new trust we have one of the most startling phenomena in the economic history of mankind. It is quite natural that it should be spoken of as constituting the "World's Greatest Revolution," while another writer [1] is forced to compare the magnitude of the operations involved to the incomprehensible figures which greet us in astronomy, in order to give us some notion of the vastness of this new corporation of corporations. Yet the thought occurs to us that we can measure astronomical forces. Can we not by analysis gain a clearer apprehension of the industrial forces which have met together and united in the United States Steel Corporation? While in human affairs we may not expect to discover the fine accuracy of astronomy, we cannot know how nearly we may approximate such exactness until we have tried.

One of the first things revealed to us by analysis is that in the steel trust we do not encounter something new in kind. The forces at work in this combination are old and familiar, and it is simply the degree in which they manifest themselves that is new. This becomes clear enough to us if we examine the kinds of industries which have been brought under unified management. What then are the kinds of industries which have been gathered together into this new trust?

Among the most prominent of these industries we find those engaged in mining operations. The appropriation of natural treasures, existing below the surface of the earth, is a chief feature in the projected work of the steel trust. These treasures are all more or less sharply limited in supply, and in many cases the limitation is such as to make

[1] Mr. Charles S. Gleed, in *Cosmopolitan Magazine*, May, 1901.

monopoly easy. In the case of the rarer treasures, or in the case of treasures with comparatively few especially fine sources of supply, we have the conditions prepared for natural monopolies of one variety. This is a mere truism. Theory and practice have for hundreds of years distinguished between these natural resources and other forms of property. The great legal systems of the world have for centuries recognized, more or less clearly, this distinction. For over six hundred years on the continent of Europe the law has, generally speaking, placed in a category by themselves natural treasures, and in 1865 Prussia passed a truly great mining law which established public property in the more important unappropriated mineral treasures in that kingdom, and did so to protect public interests. Even in this country where we are somewhat slow to recognize public as opposed to private rights, this distinction is not unknown, and in fact, in an important case in Indiana, involving the waste of natural gas, property in this natural treasure was most sharply discriminated by the Supreme Court of that state from other forms of property. Among the theoretical writers who have recognized this distinction Professor Henry C. Adams may be mentioned, who has some instructive observations on this subject in his book on " Finance."

Many manufacturing processes are included in the work of the steel trust, especially, of course, the manufacture of iron and steel. If space were not too limited, it would be worth while to quote in full from the charter the objects for which the United States Steel Corporation was formed. We note among these objects the following : " To apply for, obtain, register, purchase, lease, or otherwise to acquire, and to hold, use, operate, and introduce, and to sell, assign, or otherwise to dispose of, any trade-marks, trade names, patents, inventions, improvements, and processes." Our analysis here reveals again the presence of monopoly, and monopoly established of design by public authority in order to promote inventions and industrial improvements. We have here to do with a union in one concern of the more important protected patents and processes in great classes of industries, and so far as these are concerned, we have clear-cut monopoly.

Among the objects for which the corporation is formed we notice, furthermore, the following : " To construct bridges, ships, boats, engines, cars, and other equipment, railroads, docks, slips, elevators, waterworks, gas-works, and electric works, viaducts, canals, and other waterways, and any other means of transportation, and to sell the same, and otherwise to dispose thereof, or to maintain and operate the same." We have here again to do with industries of which the non-competitive character has long been clearly recognized ; in other words, we once more find ourselves in the field of monopoly. Moreover, it has long been known that many other businesses, especially manufacturing businesses, stand in such dependent relations to these non-competitive businesses that the latter can extend their monopolistic character to fields which otherwise would be competitive in nature. This is especially the case with transportation agencies, for, by special rates, they can easily build up favored businesses as monopolies. In fact, even unwittingly, favoritism may creep in and form monopoly. It is only through the most scrupulous impartiality like that of high-minded and disinterested judges, having ever in mind the danger of monopoly, that equality of opportunity for competitors can be maintained. Let us but reflect on the following as ways in which inequality of opportunity in transportation may arise; (*a*) general facilities, as supplying cars to one competitor more promptly than to another; (*b*) rushing through the freight of the favored shipper while that of another is sidetracked; (*c*) furnishing better terminal facilities to one person than to another; (*d*) maintenance of such relations between various modes of shipment — as for example, between tank-cars and barrels, and between rail, water, and pipe-line transportation — that advantages come to some which others do not enjoy; (*e*) classifications of freight made and changed to the advantage of favored classes; (*f*) making discriminations in favor of geographical sections in the interest of classes of shippers.

Unless in all the particulars named we maintain rigid impartiality like that of the clerk at the stamp-window of the post-office in selling stamps, it is hard to say where we shall find the limits of monopoly fifty years from now.

Is it conceivable that even excellent men, even those who in their expenditures show strongly marked philanthropic traits and tendencies, will of their own motion endeavor to maintain competitive equality of opportunity for themselves and for others? We have a rapidly growing unification of coal-carrying and coal-mining interests. May we expect that the coal-carriers will in every particular treat independent producers as well as they do themselves in their capacity as coal-producers? Was it one of the purposes of this consolidation to maintain rigid impartiality, and thus competitive equality of opportunity? If not, what then?

In casting about for an answer to these questions, our attention is attracted by a certain general restlessness on the part of the public which has invaded even Wall Street. The consumers of the country believe that monopoly exists and is expanding rapidly, and it is their conviction, as well as that of our courts, that monopoly price must mean high price — that if now it means in some cases low price, this is a mere temporary arrangement. Other producers tremble when they contemplate a billion-dollar trust with which they must have relations. The wage-earner feels that, isolated and alone, he is a pygmy, a nothing, when his individual interests are pitted against amalgamated hundreds of millions, and he is zealous in the formation of labor unions to prepare for conflict. When the citizen reflects on what is readily observable at our various seats of government, he feels that the potentialities of political power residing in a billion-dollar trust are vague, but certainly vast, perhaps illimitable.

It may be said that we are here speaking about psychical states, but psychical states are dynamic forces of society. They deserve the most careful and candid consideration on the part of the publicist.

The fact of tremendous power concentrated in the hands of the billion-dollar trust is clearly recognized. We find in this billion-dollar trust three distinct kinds of monopolistic forces working together and strengthening each other, viz., those proceeding from sharp limitations of supply of valuable minerals; those proceeding from patents and secret processes; and finally those coming from transportation agencies and other similar monopolistic pursuits. We find thus what we may call monopoly raised to the third power. On the other hand, all sources of supply are not as yet embraced in this combination, and potentialities of competition still exist here and there, but if untoward events do not beset the course of the billion-dollar steel trust, its monopolistic power is likely to increase.

We then have to do with a union of men of very exceptional but probably not unique ability, who give economic direction to a considerable percentage of the productive forces — including labor and capital — of the entire United States. Property in its nature means exclusive right of control, and these men have in their hands these exclusive rights. But our bread, our subsistence, comes from the operation of productive economic forces. Have those who draw this bread from these unified productive forces a power which brings about that equilibrium which maintains interdependence and independence? We remember what Shakespeare said about economic control: —

"You take my house when you do take the prop
That doth sustain my house ; you take my life
When you do take the means whereby I live."

While the fact of unprecedented power is admitted by our editorial writers, the hope is generally expressed that it will be used wisely, and sometimes dark hints are given as to what may follow if this power is misused. Our magnates have again and again been impressively told that the tremendousness of their power is almost appalling, and we are then reassured by grave utterances concerning the sobering effect of power. At bottom, protection is sought in the appeal to good will — to the benevolence of our industrial conquerors, our economic Alexanders and Cæsars. What are the lessons of history? Does past experience teach us that we may place our hope for economic well-being wholly or in part in the benevolence of any class of men, even the most estimable? Or, turning to the deductive argu-

213

ment, does our observation of human nature, even at the best, lead us to think this is a safe procedure? When we question ourselves, do we think we could stand such a test? Noteworthy and impressive in this connection is the following utterance of the late Benjamin Harrison: "The man whose protection from wrong rests wholly upon the benevolence of another man or of a congress is a slave — a man without rights."

III. *Remedies*

If we are not quite satisfied with appeals to benevolence, or even to an enlightened self-interest, that looks ahead and endeavors to avoid remote and long-delayed evils, we must pursue our quest for remedies farther.

One of the first things to be asked is this: Admitting that appeals to individuals and exhortation addressed to the great ones of the industrial world may produce gratifying individual action, is it possible that such individual action can produce a social system? There seems to be a growing conviction on the part of the general public that such is not the case; and in this growing conviction is to be found the explanation of the gratifying fact that we are able to find no general inclination to blame the men who have played a leading rôle in the vast industrial combinations of the present time. The general public is awed, almost dazed, by the stupendousness of industrial events, but reproaches are not hurled against our economic kings. Mr. Tom L. Johnson, mayor of Cleveland, is reported to have said in Congress that as a private citizen he would take advantage of conditions favorable to monopoly, but that so far from aiding to pass laws calculated to build up monopoly, he would do all in his power to defeat any proposals for new laws of this character, and would likewise exert himself to secure the repeal of existing law calculated to promote monopoly. There is a general inclination to believe that this is a sound and thoroughly ethical course of action ; and one finds oneself wondering at times how many of our magnates are socialists at heart, working out as best they can their theories.

Our presentation of remedies must depend upon the kind of society in which we believe. Do we desire an essentially competitive order of society ? If so, we should remember that if competition is to be maintained permanently and to work smoothly, with absence of bitterness and industrial warfare, the number of competitors must be large. Farmers cannot combine into one monopolistic group because there are too many of them, and for that same reason one farmer does not feel that personal blame attaches to his neighbor for the low price of wheat. This consideration of numbers is one important method of determining where we may and where we may not have competition. We see then one reason why in the case of the transportation agencies, gas-works, and many other kinds of business, we must have monopoly, with an option only between public and private monopoly.

Let us, then, in the fewest possible words, consider the nature of effective remedies for the evils of monopolies and trusts. First of all, we must not place the slightest confidence in any measures which forbid the growth of business or combinations on the part of persons engaged in business when they find it advantageous for them to enter into combinations. The so-called anti-trust legislation of the American commonwealths has produced harm and can produce nothing but harm. So far from lessening the concentration of production, it has rather increased it. Looser forms of combination in the face of anti-trust legislation have made way for closer and more effective unions. How these are to be prevented while the laws of private property are still maintained, is something which it is not easy to understand. Nor is it easy to see precisely what it is hoped will be accomplished by the sort of legislation which has been tried in so many of our states, and also by our federal government, with the possible exception of the federal legislation of 1903. It does not at all deal with causes, but touches only surface phenomena. We must go down far enough to reach underlying causes if we would accomplish any results.

Among remedies, first of all mention must be made of education. General education should be so developed as to prepare every boy and girl for life. The same earnest attention should be

given by our commonwealths to the education of
our youth for civic life which Germany gives to
the preparation of her young men for military
life. If the best brains of the country were earnestly devoted to the preparation of our young
people for civic life, and if money were as freely
expended for this preparation as in Germany for
the army, we should have wonderful results. We
have a struggle for life. This it is not desirable to
abolish. It is desirable to give for it the most
thorough preparation. But in addition to general
education a training in economics is needed which
will lift to a higher plane our economic discussions
and will render impossible the serious consideration which is so often given among us to quack
remedies for economic evils.

In the second place, we must take up earnestly
the problem of natural monopolies. The time has
gone by for a discussion of the question, Shall
monopolies be publicly controlled or not? The
principle of control is accepted by every thinking
person and is a well-recognized principle of jurisprudence in every civilized land. The question
which has not been fully decided is this : Shall we
have public control of private property interests in
undertakings which fall under the head of natural
monopolies, or shall social control be an outcome
of public property with public management? To
put it more concretely : Shall we have private gas-
works with a state gas commission to exercise
control over them, as in Massachusetts, or shall

we have municipal gas-works and allow social control to proceed naturally and spontaneously from municipal ownership and management? Shall we maintain our private railways and attempt to control them through a further development of state railway commissions and the Interstate Commerce Commission, or shall we have public ownership with public operation? We must take the one alternative or the other, and either one is beset with immense difficulties. In either case the ends to be achieved are similar, and there is not so much room for controversy concerning these ends as there is for controversy concerning the methods whereby they are to be attained.

We must bring it about that those who own and manage such businesses as gas-works, railways, and the like, — that is, if we are to retain private property in these enterprises, — have no advantage over those engaged in other kinds of business. We must have no privileged classes composed of monopolists. We must not think that in the abolition of politically privileged classes we have accomplished the abolition of special privileges.

Economic privileges are of greater significance than political privileges, and we may have privileged classes although they do not go by the name of duke and lord; they may be simply magnates and kings, as gas magnates and railway kings. Through social control property and enterprise invested in monopolistic businesses must be placed on the same footing with property and enterprise invested in competitive businesses. It is idle to claim that such is the case now, when franchises for which no one has toiled in any honorable and legitimate way yield to their owners millions upon millions of dollars of unearned wealth.

In the next place, it must be brought about that those who have dealings with monopolistic enterprises are fairly and impartially treated. Tyranny and oppression, whether directed against the general public or employees, must be abolished. War must be waged upon monopolies founded on private favoritism until they become a thing of the past. They must take their place in history alongside of monopolies granted by Tudor kings to their favorites.

The third class of remedies is found in the regulation of the transmission of property from generation to generation, and this must be brought about in part by taxation, in part by laws which aim otherwise to secure a wide diffusion of wealth. This subject will be considered more fully in the chapter devoted to the inheritance of property.[1]

Tariff reform is mentioned as a fourth remedy, although the present author attaches far less importance to it than many others do. Wherever monopoly clearly rests upon the tariff, however, he is prepared to indorse a reform of the tariff.

The fifth measure of reform which is recom-

[1] Pt. II, Ch. VII.

EVOLUTION OF INDUSTRIAL SOCIETY

mended is the reform of the patent law. Not an
abolition, be it understood, but such a reform along
well approved lines as will render patents of less
significance as a foundation of monopolies. It is
quite practicable to accomplish this end and still
maintain a patent system which will afford as great
a stimulus to invention as does our present patent
law. There are many different ways of encourag-
ing and rewarding invention outside our patent
system, but the most conservative proposition for
meeting the situation is that of a former Commissioner of Patents, who would have the government
reserve the right to purchase patents and throw
them open to public use. In this connection, it is
well to call attention to an impressive occurrence
which took place two years ago in Madison,
Wisconsin, when the legislature of that state presented a medal to Professor S. M. Babcock, of the
State University, on account of his valuable inventions, especially the " Babcock milk test," worth
millions annually to the farmers of this country,
which he had refused to have patented, because
he felt that as a public servant he ought to give
the general public the benefits of his inventions.

The sixth line of reform is one which is still
more important, and that is the reform of the law
of private corporations. As coöperation takes
place so largely through private corporations,
which afford to persons of the smallest means
opportunities for participation in the largest enterprises, there is no ground for sympathy with any

proposal to abolish or limit private corporations. What is desired is to bring them under effective public control, in order to secure honesty and promote individual responsibility. Several things are needed to accomplish this purpose. One is complete publicity, with such extension of the criminal law as would send to the penitentiary as quickly the man guilty of theft through the medium of a corporation as the man guilty of theft in his individual capacity. We need, for effective control, bureaus of corporations in our states, as well as an interstate bureau of corporations, such as that which has been established in connection with the new federal Department of Commerce and Labor. As a model for the general law of incorporation, the national banking act is recommended, although it is recognized that to adapt this to manufacturing and commercial purposes a few minor changes are necessary. One special purpose of this reform of private corporations is to protect the investor and increase the number of investors and thus promote a wide diffusion of property. Private corporations own a very large proportion of the wealth of the country, and if their management is of such a nature that the ordinary man can neither understand nor trust it, the consequence must be to confine the corporate ownership of property with its advantages to relatively few people, and the further consequence of this condition must be the encouragement of socialism, which means the abandonment of the effort to secure diffused prosperity through private property in productive capital.

Public opinion has during the past two or three years made gratifying progress in its attitude toward monopolies and trusts. At no time during the past twenty years has there been less blind denunciation of mere combination and large-scale industry; at no previous time during this period has it been so clearly seen by so many people that the real evil against which we must contend is monopoly. Finally, never before in the United States have we had such intelligent legislation on the subject of monopolies and trusts as that enacted in 1903 by Congress. Direct opposition to combinations has been at least partially abandoned, and an effort is now to be made to exercise control over monopolistic undertakings, with the end of doing away with private favoritism as a basis of monopoly. Congress has adopted in its legislation the view, expressed by Attorney-General Knox, that monopoly is the evil against which we contend and that monopoly rests upon special privileges which may be abolished so as thereby to bring us nearer the goal of equality of opportunities. It remains to be seen whether or not the remedies proposed are adequate; especially whether or not it is possible to control effectively the gigantic corporations which rest upon a basis of natural monopoly. In the meantime we are gathering experience which will give us more light on the problems presented by monopolies and trusts.

MONOPOLIES AND TRUSTS

LITERATURE

Of many references which could be given, a few books only will be mentioned.

BAKER, CHAS. WHITING, Monopolies and the People. 3d ed. New York, 1899. An interesting work in which the author attempts to formulate the laws of competition.

BOLEN, GEORGE L., The Plain Facts as to the Trusts and the Tariff. New York, 1903. This is a popular work, giving much valuable information. Quotations from many different sources, presenting a variety of opinions, constitute a special feature of the book.

Chicago Conference on Trusts. Chicago, 1900. This gives the proceedings of the most important gathering as yet held for the discussion of trusts. The Conference was held in Chicago September, 1899. It presents the views of many leading thinkers upon the subject, and gives a general survey of the field which is not easily found elsewhere.

CLARK, JOHN B., The Control of Trusts. New York, 1902. The idea of Professor Clark is that the only dangerous element in the trusts is the power of monopoly, and that this can be removed or regulated.

ELY, RICHARD T., Monopolies and Trusts. New York, 1900. The distinctive feature of this book is the attention given to the theory of monopoly, the author holding that the combinations called trusts cannot profitably be discussed until monopoly is correctly defined and its significance understood.

GUNTON, GEORGE, Trusts and the Public. New York, 1899. A presentation of the subject from the point of view friendly to the trusts. The author, however, makes a distinction between good trusts and bad trusts, and is by no means an indiscriminate advocate.

JENKS, J. W., The Trust Problem. New York, 1900. The author favors the control of trusts, and presents in this little book a great deal of information which he gathered while serving as the expert agent of the United States Industrial Commission and as consulting expert of the United States Department of Labor.

LLOYD, HENRY D., Wealth against Commonwealth. New York, 1894. An arraignment of the Standard Oil Trust.

MACROSTY, HENRY W., Trusts and the State. A Sketch of Competition. London, 1901. The author of this book is a Fabian socialist, and like the socialists in general fails to distinguish adequately between what is simply large-scale production and monopolistic production. The socialist finds monopoly everywhere, and thinks it is only a matter of time when every branch of production will be fully monopolized. This view colors the treatment of trusts by socialists. The present work, however, is one which, notwithstanding these defects, is worthy of careful study, especially on account of the information which it gives concerning English industry.

NETTLETON, A. B., Trusts or Competition. Chicago, 1900. Quotations are given presenting both sides of the question.

United States Industrial Commission, Report of. Washington, 1900. Vol. I, Trusts and Industrial Combinations. Vol. II, Trusts and Corporation Laws. Vol. XIII, Industrial Combinations. Vol. XIX, Miscellaneous (giving a review of the treatment in the earlier volumes). This gives the results of the most important investigation of the subject as yet made under the direction of public authority.

CHAPTER V

I. *Municipal Ownership of Natural Monopolies*

THE question under discussion relates to the ownership and management of those local businesses which furnish what are called public utilities. The principal classes of these public utilities are water, light, and transportation. They are called monopolies because, as we know from experience, we cannot have in their case effective and permanent competition.

It is often said that we do not want to decide the question of municipal ownership in accordance with general principles, but that each case should be decided as it arises. If New York City desires public ownership of waterworks, it is urged, let New York City by all means try the experiment; but let New Haven, if the people of that city so desire, continue private ownership of waterworks. Still others say, let us adhere to private ownership until we find that we have made a serious mistake in so doing. Both these attitudes imply the renunciation of science, or a denial of the possibility of a scientific solution of the problem. Imagine such an attitude in engineering as applied, let us say, to bridge-building. The result would surely be disaster. The outcome of this attitude in what we may call applied economics or social engineering has likewise been disastrous. Mistakes have been made which it has not been possible to correct, or which have been corrected with great loss. The private ownership of water-works in London, which still persists, although recognized to be an evil many years ago, affords an illustration. If at length this evil is corrected, it will cost the taxpayers many millions of dollars which might have been saved. Innumerable illustrations could be afforded, did space permit. What must be desired by any one who has an appreciation of the nature of modern science, is the establishment of general principles whereby mistakes may be avoided and loss prevented. The practical man will naturally take into account the actual, concrete condition in his application of general principles. The social engineer must, in this particular, follow the practice of the mechanical engineer.

When we approach the question of public ownership *versus* private ownership of great industries as those connected with artificial light and transportation, our attention is attracted by the municipal corruption which exists, particularly in our own country. The fact of this municipal corruption, and also the further fact of the very general incompetency in the management of municipal affairs, are not called in question, and they are not under discussion. The corruption and incompetency may not everywhere be so bad as many pessimists imagine, and it may, furthermore, be true that, in both respects, we have in many cities witnessed gratifying improvement. Yet when we have made these admissions, the true state of the case is bad enough. The civic conscience with us is slow of development. The satisfactory performance of public duties implies, in some particulars, a higher civilization than we have reached. It requires some development of the imagination to see the harm and suffering brought to countless individuals by lapses in civic virtue. Furthermore, it implies a higher development of conscience than that now generally found among us, to reach that state in which there is a conscious desire to abstain from all acts which may hurt people who are not seen. Many a man will give to a poor widow, whom he sees, money to relieve her distress, but, at the same time, will not hesitate to increase the burdens of poor widows whom he does not see, by fraudulent evasion of taxation.[1]

The men now in our municipal councils are not the kind of men to whom we would gladly turn over vast business interests. The very

[1] The slow development of social ethics is admirably described in " Democracy and Social Ethics," by Jane Addams.

thought repels us. Whether or not they are morally better or worse than the men who in many cases are said to corrupt them, and who now exercise an important influence in the management of privately owned public utilities, it is freely conceded that they are less fit for the conduct of important businesses. We want street railways managed by men who understand the street railway business, gas-works managed by men who understand the gas business, and neither class of enterprises managed by men whose gifts are most conspicuous in the partisan manipulation of ward politics. It is important that it should be understood that the advocates of municipal ownership do not call in question the fact of municipal corruption and inefficiency in the management of public business, and that they have no desire to turn over the management of public utilities to a class of men who must still be considered typical in the municipal council of the great American city.

But when we have admitted freely corruption and inefficiency in municipal government, it still remains to examine into the causes of these conditions, for there is a very widespread suspicion that a large share of the responsibility therefor must be laid at the door of private ownership. A real, vital question is this: Would we have the same class of men in our common councils which we now find there, should public ownership replace private ownership? Is it true that private ownership places in office and keeps in office some of our worst municipal wrongdoers? It is important that the reader should understand the real nature of the problem under discussion, and it is believed that these questions which have just been asked bring before us a large part of that problem. This important problem, the solution of which is of national significance, should be approached with no partisan bias, and no angry recriminations or denunciations should be tolerated. The spirit of the injunction, "Come, let us reason together," should be the spirit of approach.

We must clearly and sharply fasten in our minds the indisputable fact that, with respect to public utilities of the sort under discussion, we are confined to one of two alternatives. These alternatives are, on the one hand, public control of private corporations, on the other, public ownership with the public control which naturally springs from ownership. The experience of the entire civilized world has established the fact that we are restricted to these alternatives. We may have private street railways, private gas-works, private waterworks, etc., but in that case it is invariably and in the very nature of the case necessary to exercise public control over their operations. Charges must be regulated, general conditions of service must be prescribed, and regulation must be found for a thousand and one cases in which public and private interests touch each other. This is because, on the one hand, the nature of the service rendered is in such a peculiar degree a public service, and also because the effective control of full and free competition is absent. We may, on the other hand, choose public ownership and management. We could, of course, separate public ownership from public management, and consider each one. In other words, we could have a publicly owned urban transportation system with private operation. Generally, public ownership and public management go together; in our present treatment we will not undertake to separate them.

It is freely granted that either one of our two alternatives presents immense difficulties. This is a further point concerning which there can be no controversy among those who really understand the nature of the case. The evolution of industrial society has again brought us problems most difficult of solution. If we may use the language of design, history teaches us that Providence does not intend that men organized in society should have what we are always looking for in the future, namely, an easy-going time. Every age has its problems. In one age they may be brought by the inroads of barbarians, in another age by famine and pestilence, in another age by international wars. We have been dreaming of a coming time when no social problems should vex society; but, if history teaches us anything, it shows us that in such dreaming we are indulging in Utopian aspirations. Every civilization has been tested heretofore, and every civilization must have its test in the future, our own included. One of the tests of our civilization is the ability to solve the problem under discussion.

The question which confronts us is this : Which one of the two alternatives promises in the long run the best results?

Those who talk glibly about public control of those private corporations owning and operating public utilities frequently exhibit a sad ignorance of what their proposed remedy for existing evils means. They think in generalities, and do not reflect upon what control means in details. We have to observe, first of all, that public control of private corporations furnishing public utilities so-called means a necessary antagonism of interests in the civic household. Human nature is such that those who are to be controlled cannot be satisfied with the control exercised. However righteous the control may be, those who are controlled will frequently feel themselves aggrieved and wronged, and will try to escape the control. It is, furthermore, a necessary outcome of human nature that those persons who are to be controlled should enter politics in order that they may either escape the control, or shape it to their own ends. Again, we must remember what vast aggregations of men and capital it is proposed to control. The men owning and operating the corporations which furnish public utilities are numerous, and they maintain large armies of employees of all social grades, from the gifted and highly trained attorney to the unskilled laborer. The amount of capital involved in a great city is counted by tens of millions. The very nature of the case brings it about that there should be persistent, never ceasing activity on the part of those to be controlled. The effort to escape from this control, or to shape it, is a part of the efforts by which men earn their livelihood, and their activity is as regular as their hunger. The efforts of patriotic and high-minded citizens, in their self-sacrificing neglect of their private affairs to look after public concerns, may grow weary, but not so the activity of the corporations to be controlled. Can a task of greater difficulty be well suggested? It is not said that the problem here presented is one which it is impossible for modern civilization to solve; but it is well that the general public should know precisely what it means. Some of us are to control others, and to do so against their will. But who are those whom we are asked to control? They are very frequently our friends and neighbors. I am asked to resist what is esteemed the extortion of a gas company; but one of the gas magnates may be my neighbor and friend, and occupy a pew next to mine in church. Perhaps the gas magnate is my employer. Perhaps he has just contributed, and with the best intent in the world, one hundred dollars to an object which I have greatly at heart. Perhaps I am a college professor, and the street-car magnate whose rapacity I am called upon to help hold in check has endowed the chair which I occupy. Imaginary illustrations can be continued indefinitely, and those who desire to do so can in any city make them sufficiently concrete. Is it strange that many of us who are called upon to control others of us should simply refuse to do it ?

It is possible in this place to do little more than to throw out suggestions. It is noteworthy that in Massachusetts public control of corporations furnishing public utilities has been tried more persistently than anywhere else, and that in that state there is a stronger sentiment than anywhere else in the Union in favor of public ownership and public management. Serious charges have been brought against the Board of Gas and Electric Lighting Commissioners, which has to exercise control over gas and electric-lighting plants. Even a paper of the standing of the *Springfield Republican* has felt called upon to rebuke the board severely for keeping secret information which it has gathered. The attitude of the board is characterized as " extraordinary." " If the board," says the *Springfield Republican*, " is empowered to keep secret what information it is pleased to, how are the people to know that they may not become a mere agency of the monopolies to cover up and justify their possible undue exactions?" Insinuations of this kind are frequently heard in Massachusetts. Dismissing all charges of corruption and bad intention, we have as a net result a strong movement in Massachusetts, away from private ownership of public utilities, to public ownership.

The writer has followed this subject, and the trend of opinion with respect to it, for fifteen years with some care. In his own judgment the trend in favor of public ownership is marked and surprising. He has seen one investigator after another start with prepossessions in favor of public control of private corporations, and turn away from that position as a hopeless one, and take up a position in favor of public ownership as the only practicable solution under our American conditions. There lies before the writer a letter recently received from an attorney, a member of a well-known firm in one of our great cities. This lawyer has been forced by experience to abandon the position in favor of private ownership. He says, as the result of long-continued and self-sacrificing efforts to improve politics in his own city: " The alleged benefits of regulation are practically as impossible as an attempt to regulate the laws of gravitation, for our legislative councils are nominated, elected, and controlled by forces too subtle and insidious to be attacked, and even to be known. . . . A community cannot regulate against millions of dollars organized to prevent it. This temptation disappears, however, when the municipality becomes the owner."

The difficulties of public ownership are not to be denied. They lie on the surface. The problem in the case of public ownership is to secure men

of talent and experience to conduct these enterprises, and keep them in office during good be-
havior; to engage men for all positions on the
basis of merit, and, while retaining vast armies of
employees, to enact such legislation and adminis-
trative reforms as will prevent employees of the
city, engaged in furnishing public utilities, from
either using their political power for their own selfish ends, or from being used for partisan purposes.
This implies, on the part of society, an appreciation of excellence of service and a thorough-going
reform of municipal civil service. Politicians of
the baser sort and all those who have selfish ends
to be gained by political corruption will work
against such reform. On the other hand, public
ownership with public operation presents the issues
in a comparatively simple form. The clarification
of issues is, indeed, one of the strong arguments
in favor of municipal ownership. Who knows to
what extent employees on the street railways of
Baltimore, Philadelphia, New York, and Chicago
are appointed through the influence of politicians?
It is known, however, that many appointments are
made through the influence of politicians of precisely the worst sort. It is furthermore known that
these corporations are now generally in politics.
But because the corporations furnishing these public utilities are owners of private property, and because they conduct a business which is only quasi-
public, the political corruption with which they are
connected is hidden and obscure, and voters are

confused and perplexed. Public ownership carries home to every one the importance of good government, and arrays on the side of good government the strong classes in a community now so often indifferent. Frequently men who are power-ful in a community, in working for good government, work against, rather than for, their own private interests. It is, indeed, gratifying to see men of wealth, as frequently as they do, turn aside from selfish considerations to promote measures calculated to advance the general welfare. But can we expect this kind of conduct persistently from the great majority? Have we any right to expect it? A personal allusion is sufficiently instructive to warrant reference to it. When the writer had invested what was for him a considerable sum in gas stock, he tried to answer for himself this question: As an owner of gas stock, exactly what kind of municipal government do I want? The government of the city in which was located the gas-works in which the writer was interested was a stench in the nostrils of reformers throughout the country: but he could not persuade himself that as an owner of gas stock any very considerable change was for his interest. The city government, as it then was, was a " safe " one, and the result of a change could not be foretold. Is not this, as a matter of fact, the solution of the problem which owners of stock in street railways, gas-works, and similar enterprises generally reach when they look at municipal reform solely from the point of view of self-interest? And can we, then, be surprised at a certain apathy and indifference on the part of what are called the "better classes" in a community? Men of great wealth have been known to work directly against their own narrow interests for the public weal, but has an entire class of men ever been known to do this?

A further result of municipal ownership would be a better balance between private and public interests, and this better balance would strengthen the existing order against the attacks of socialists and anarchists, on the one hand, and unscrupulous plutocrats, on the other. A balance between private and public enterprise is what is fundamental in our present social order, and a disturbance of this balance consequently threatens this order. This balance is favorable to liberty, which is threatened when it is disturbed either in the one direction or the other. Any one who follows passing events with care cannot fail to see that it is menaced by socialism, on the one hand, and by plutocracy, on the other. A man of high standing in Philadelphia, himself a man of large wealth, when presiding at a public meeting recently, stated, practically in so many words, that a professor in a school of some note had lost his position on account of a monograph which he wrote in relation to the street railways of that city. This monograph was temperate in tone, and its scholarly character elicited commendation on all sides. We need not go into the merits of this particular case, but we cannot fail to notice disquieting rumors in regard to the attacks upon freedom of speech, which are an outcome of private ownership of public utilities. There is a widespread apprehension that the utterance of opinion upon one side promotes one's interest, and that the utterance of opinion upon the other side may prove damaging. Mathematical proof cannot well be adduced, but readers can, by careful observation, reach a conclusion as to the question whether or not our industrial order is menaced by plutocracy, always bearing in mind that plutocracy does not mean honestly gotten and honestly administered wealth. There are good rich men, and bad rich men, as there are good poor men, and bad poor men. Does private ownership of public utilities, on the one hand, tempt rich men to wrong courses of action, and does it, on the other hand, place great power in the hands of unscrupulous wealth?

In the restricted space of the present essay it is impossible to go statistically into experience. The question may be raised, however, Has any one ever noticed an improvement in municipal government from a lessening of the functions of municipal government? Can any one point to a municipal government which has improved because its duties have been diminished, and the number of its employees lessened? If we turn away from local government, do we find that it is through the lessening of the function of government in general that an improvement is achieved? At one time, the Italian government operated the Italian railways. Later it leased the railways to a private corporation. Has this retirement of Italy from the operation of the railways produced a regeneration in public life? As we travel over this country, and observe the course of local government, do we not, on the contrary, find that, on the whole, it has improved as its functions have increased, and as it appeals directly and effectively to larger and larger numbers? The case of England is a very clear one. If we go back fifty years, we shall probably find that the government of English cities was quite as bad as ours is now. During the past fifty years there has been a continuous improvement, and this has accompanied continual expansion of municipal activity, while at the same time, through an extension of the suffrage, English municipal government has become increasingly democratic in character. We must hesitate about establishing a causal connection between these two movements, but is it unnatural to suppose that there may be such a connection? When there is a great deal at stake, when the city has much to do, good government of the cities appeals to all right-minded persons; and if there is no division of interests through private ownership, we ought, in a civilized community, to expect to find all honest and intelligent people working together for good government. A tangible basis is afforded the masses for an appeal for their own higher interests, and reliance is placed upon municipal self-help. Instead of asking great private corporations to do things for them, the people are told to help themselves.

Mistakes and wrongdoing must be anticipated under either one of our two possible systems. What about the relative seriousness of the mistakes and wrongdoing, however? We have a certain demoralization in each case, and a certain loss. While in the case of public ownership we have an opportunity to recover from mistaken action, in the case of private ownership mistaken and wrong action is often irretrievable in its consequences. Take the case of New York City as an illustration. Jacob Sharp secured a franchise for the Broadway surface railway through wholesale corruption, and was sent to the penitentiary. The franchise, however, was retained by those into whose hands it fell, and others have entered into the fruits of his theft. Under our American system of government, in cases of this sort, stolen goods are retained. The franchises are retained and the forgotten millions continue to suffer, because their rights have not been adequately safeguarded. With the other policy, namely, that of public ownership, how different would be the result? If the street railways were mismanaged, or their earnings stolen, it would be sufficient to turn out the municipal plunderers. Too many overlook what is distinctively American in our problem; namely, our constitutional system, which protects franchise grants when once made, and

so renders irretrievable a mistaken policy, provided we have the system of private ownership.

Let it be distinctly understood that the position
is not taken by the present writer in favor of
municipal ownership at any and all times, and
everywhere and under all circumstances. It must
come in the right way, it must come deliberately,
and it must come provided with adequate safe-
guards. It must come as a part of other movements, especially of full civil service reform. But
it is calculated in itself to promote these other reforms, and in some cases municipal ownership will
be the first step in the direction of that full civil
service reform which is so sadly needed.[1] In
some cases civilization may be in too low a condition to permit municipal ownership. The socializa-

[1] A few years ago a successful candidate for the mayoralty in
Des Moines, Iowa, made this statement in his campaign: " If
elected, I expect to continue in my attempts to carry out the principles of my platform of two years ago, reiterated in the platform
of this year, for the public ownership and control of public utilities
such as water, gas and electric light plants, street railways and telephones. . . . I should like to see a civil service law enacted to go
hand in hand with these reforms, but I do not believe that we should
wait for such a measure. I am firmly of the opinion that the public
ownership of such franchises will of itself bring about civil service
reform. Municipal ownership will do more than any other one
thing to improve city government in America. In my opinion
much of the poor and bad government in city affairs is due to the
influence of franchise-holding corporations. It is to their interest
to have poor government, to secure the election and appointment
of officials whom they can control to their selfish ends. We have
seen examples of this in our own city, where local corporations
exerted their influence against salutary measures looking toward
civil service and other similar reforms."

tion of public sentiment which must lie back of proper social action may not have gone far enough. The question is: Have we the social man back of the social action which we advocate? If we are talking about the heart of Africa, with its individualistic blacks, unquestionably we have not the social man who would make possible any considerable amount of social action. Among barbarians and semi-civilized people the few must do things for the many. Social action must not be forced down from above, and it must not come accidentally, if it is to be successful. It must come as the result of full and free discussion, and of full and free expression on the part of the people. It is on this account that the initiative and referendum, in a country like ours, may properly accompany the social action. Have we in our own country the social man to back social action? If he does not everywhere exist, he is coming, and coming rapidly, and the amount of social action which the socialization of sentiment makes possible and desirable increases in proportion as he makes his appearance. The question of municipal ownership is a question of social psychology. It turns on the nature of the social mind.

II. *Note on the Establishment of a Parcels Post, and the National Ownership of the Telephone Telegraph, and Railways.*

The question naturally arises to what extent are the arguments which have been adduced in favor of municipal ownership of natural monopolies applicable to monopolistic businesses which operate on a national scale, and which, therefore, must be owned and managed by the nation, if public ownership is to replace private ownership. This is a large question, and here and now it is proposed simply to bring forward a few pertinent suggestions which naturally connect themselves with the treatment of local monopolies.

The first three undertakings mentioned do not offer special difficulties, and the arguments in favor of municipal ownership would, in the main, hold with reference to them. The post-office, even with all its imperfections, is serving the people of the United States admirably. Generally speaking, one finds courteous and considerate treatment accorded to the public by the officials, which frequently is in pleasing contrast to the brusqueness of the officials of great private monopolistic corporations. The effort made to serve the public and to see that mail reaches its correct destination is remarkable. If any kind of clew is given, the person to whom a letter is addressed generally receives it, even if the address is incorrect. The writer, while in Baltimore, has received letters which were directed to him in Boston, and the success of the post-office in finding persons is sometimes almost wonderful.[1] This furnishes marked

1 Since writing the above the author has received a letter addressed, "Richard T. Ely, Johns Hopkins University, Stanford, Cal."

contrast with the very slight effort on the part of express companies to find persons, and their frequent indifference about addresses, as they do not generally have any system of keeping them. When a telegraph or express company finds difficulty about an address, a postal card is put in the post-office addressed as the message or parcel is, and the post-office generally finds the person. This is only one of many illustrations which could be adduced.

Many of the defects in the post-office are frequently attributed, by those who should know, to the interested efforts of private persons to prevent a satisfactory development of this branch of the public service. The rate of one cent an ounce for merchandise is high, and the rate of one cent a pound for periodicals, when sent out by publishers, seems too low. What is needed is an arrangement whereby parcels up to, say, fifteen pounds can be sent through the post-office, with a charge which will cover expenses. In Germany the charge for a parcel sent to any part of the German Empire is twelve cents for any weight up to something like ten pounds. It has been claimed that on this part of the post-office business there is a loss in Germany, and with our greater distances and the high charges exacted from the post-office by the railways a higher rate would be required. But a rate which covers cost would be far less than that now exacted by the express companies, and altogether apart from that would be the convenience of reaching the entire country, and the service would be unified. This is an important consideration, because in the case of each one of the services which we are now discussing, unity of management is one of the conditions of excellence in service. Other things being equal, the nearer the approximation to unity the better the service. About the importance of the parcels post there will probably be little difference of opinion on the part of competent persons who are strictly impartial.

The telephone service is largely local, but the long-distance service becomes of increasing importance, and with the extension of the long-distance service and a decrease in charges its relative importance would increase still further. This is something which is readily appreciated by those who enjoy what is essentially a local service by a local company. Many of the smaller cities in the United States now have local companies which compete with the so-called Bell telephone with its national connections. The local service is frequently excellent and charges low, but the great national company is able to maintain its existence on account of its far wider connections. It is obvious to every one with experience that unity in the telephone service is a consideration of decisive importance, so much so that it is likely to be secured ultimately either by private or public action. The only method of securing the unified service and the extensions which are desirable, with low charges,

is through government ownership, which has worked
well wherever it has been tried. As a means of
communication it naturally belongs to the post-
office, and can advantageously be operated in connection therewith. The farmers are beginning to
appreciate the importance of the telephone, and are
urging its extension as a means of removing the
isolation of farm life. There are good reasons for
believing that the telephone can be so extended
throughout our rural districts as to render life in
the country far more attractive, and to promote
the intelligence of the farming class. This is a
general social consideration which constitutes a
strong argument for the national ownership of the
telephone.

The telegraph service is similar in character, and
along with the telephone could advantageously be
operated as a part of the postal system of the
country. It is simply a quicker method of trans-
mitting intelligence than the letter. Every great
civilized country, outside the United States, enjoys
the advantage of public ownership of the telegraph,
and in European countries, roughly speaking, the
charges for messages are from ten cents to fifteen
cents, regardless of distance. For twelve cents a
message can be sent from one end of the German
Empire to the other, and for many of these messages in this country a charge of at least fifty cents
would be exacted. The figures which attempt to
show low charges for sending telegrams in the
United States are entirely unscientific and mis-

leading. Quite often a long distance is taken in this country and is compared with a similar long distance in Europe, although this long distance in Europe means an international telegram which has to pass over four or five countries, and frequently will also include cable service. It must be borne in mind that distance has relatively little to do with the cost of telegraphing, but the cost and charges are naturally increased in the case of international telegrams, especially when cable service is involved. Altogether apart from this is the superior excellence of the service under government ownership, about which no person who has lived in a country like England or Germany is likely to be in doubt. It is also important in this connection to consider the condition of the employees. The lot of the telegraph employees in this country in our great cities can easily be ascertained by observation and inquiry. The offices are frequently in basements where the sanitary conditions are far from being the best. Employees are very largely young boys on small pay, who are in great danger of suffering contamination on account of the places to which they are sent. The standard of admission to the service is very low, and in the vast majority of cases the service leads to no desirable future for those engaged in it. This is in marked contrast with the conditions in our post-office and also with the conditions which obtain, generally speaking, where we have government ownership. There lies before the writer a review of two books which gives instructions and directions for those who are preparing for the examination for admission to the telegraph or telephone service in the post-office of the German Empire. It appears that the qualifications imply a considerable acquisition of knowledge and some natural ability. The telegraph officials have to pass examinations, not only in telegraphy, but also in physics, chemistry, geography, and mathematics. Those who enter these services find in them a career. The service is also performed under wholesome conditions by persons of suitable age, so that we have better moral and physical conditions of employment for a great body of men as a result of government ownership. We have in consequence, to be sure, higher expenses, but a decrease in human costs.

When we come to a treatment of railways, new considerations of vast importance enter into the discussion. Very generally when the nationalization of railways is mentioned, the difficulties connected with the civil service are adduced as an argument against nationalization. This argument, while important, is not conclusive. We have the fact of the present interference of railways in politics. We have also the possibilities of organizing railway employees on a more or less military basis and protecting them and the general public from the dangers connected with partisan politics. It is interesting in this connection to remember what Bismarck said about the employees of the Prussian railways and the influence of the government over them when the Prussian Parliament was debating the purchase of private lines in 1879–1880. He made the point that at that time it was very easy for the government to secure the votes of railway employees through arrangements with the officers of the railway. The railways, he stated, continually desired something of the government, and were always willing to pay in votes of railway employees for the desired concession. After the railways had been purchased, he said that the employees would at least have the protection of the civil service law, whereas then they had nothing. It is believed that a careful examination of all the factors which enter into the nationalization of the railways, including the psychical factors, will show that the difficulties connected with the employment of so large a number of men by the government have been unduly magnified, although it is plain that a grave problem in this particular does exist.

The most serious objection against the government ownership of railways is connected with the question of rates. Every change in rates means a change in the relative advantages of one part of the country as compared with another part of the country. Every city in the country is now striving in one way or another for a change in rates which will help it, and sometimes this is an increase in rates in order to bring to one city business which at present is carried on elsewhere. Not long ago, the merchants of a Wisconsin city made vigorous protests against the low passenger charges to Chicago in order to keep the people in the city from going to Chicago to purchase supplies of various kinds. Under national ownership and management of the railways there would be a continual struggle of section with section for advantageous rates, and unless the rate problem could be worked out in some simple, easily comprehended way which would commend itself to the public at large, this struggle of section with section could scarcely fail to prove disastrous. No one can tell what the outcome of this sectionalism might be. But what we can see in regard to the pressure of each section of the country, at the present time, to secure advantages from federal legislation, and the frequent shocking disregard displayed by one section for the interests of other sections or of the country as a whole, must lead to very grave apprehensions concerning the result of sectional struggles in the adjustment of railway freight and passenger rates, especially, however, of freight rates. This is the most serious obstacle in the way of nationalization of railways, and brings before us different considerations from those which are decisive in the case of local monopolies, or the post-office, telegraph, or telephone.

It can indeed be argued that we have the rate problem with us as a very troublesome problem at the present time, and that through the Interstate Commerce Commission the national government participates in the solution of this question. This is all true, but it is certain that at the present time we do not have that kind of a sectional struggle which we must fear under government ownership. Perhaps the greatest single danger in the private ownership of railways is that it tends first to form classes, and then to array class against class. It forms classes in the very nature of the case. First we have the classes in the railway service. About one per cent of those engaged in the service are officers and the rest employees, and the contrasts among these employees in remuneration and in conditions of employment are vast, and, whether they ought to do so or not, do have a tendency to cultivate bitterness and class division. Under government employment the differences would be diminished by improving the condition of the ordinary employees and by lessening the salaries received by those occupying the higher positions. Sanitary conditions would be improved, and the dangers connected with the service would be diminished, for the government could not withstand the agitation for improvement as private corporations can. The most important question in this connection is whether or not the clamor on the part of employees would not result in an undue shortening of hours, and a disproportionate increase in the wages of the employees. There is also a question whether the clamor for reduced rates might not push down the rates to a point where they would be unremunerative and fail to cover expenses of operation. We have, then, as a favorable aspect of the influence of the voters in the case of government railways the removal of dangers and improvement otherwise in the conditions surrounding railway employment; on the other hand, we have the danger that the government could not stop at the right point in the adjustment of wages and hours of service, and also in lowering charges for freight and passenger service.

But there is still another way in which the private ownership of railways tends to class formation, and that is through the favoritism shown to individuals in the community, which is largely responsible for the bad features of the trust movement. Everywhere throughout the United States we can find manufacturers and shippers who have been favored, and if there are any favored it is necessarily at the expense of others. We have favored classes, and this tends to promote class formation and to incite one class to hate another. In conclusion, then, we have as the chief count against public ownership of railways the danger of sectionalism, and as the chief count against the private ownership of railways the fact that private ownership encourages the formation of classes and an increasing estrangement of the classes when they are formed. At the present time the danger of sectionalism would seem to be more serious than the other danger. Whichever alternative we take, it is possible to effect improvement and to devise means to lessen the evils which are incident to the form of ownership selected. Private railways can be controlled if government is strong and pure enough for this control. Wages and conditions of service, as well as rates, can be adjusted under government ownership if government is strong and pure enough to devise right standards and to resist popular clamor.

LITERATURE

While a great deal has been written on the subject of this chapter, it will generally be conceded that it is for the most part entirely unsatisfactory. There are, however, some exceptions. All recent text-books of economics deal with this subject in what is considered its proper place. In addition to these text-books, it is sufficient for the purposes of the present chapter to call attention to a few other works.

BEMIS, EDWARD W., and others, Municipal Monopolies. New York, 1899. This book is altogether the best work on the subject; with which it deals.

HADLEY, ARTHUR T., Railroad Transportation; its History and its Laws. New York, 1885. A scientific treatment of the subject; unfriendly to national ownership.

HUDSON, JAMES R., The Railways and the Republic. New York, 1886. A sharp arraignment of the railway management of the United States, with proposal of public ownership of the road-bed with private and competing operation; a plan which finds few, if any, advocates at the present time. The chief value of this work is its criticism of railway management.

MEYER, B. H., Railway Legislation in the United States. New York, 1903. Gives results of regulation in the United States.

In addition to books, mention may be made of Municipal Affairs, published by the Reform Club Committee on City Affairs, 52 William Street, New York City. This is altogether the best magazine which deals with the various phases of municipal government, and has many excellent articles on the subject of municipal ownership.

ATE